Approaching the Passion

Approaching the Revision

Approaching the Passion

Words of Reflection

With study questions
by Elizabeth McQuoid

Authentic

MILTON KEYNES • COLORADO SPRINGS • HYDERABAD

First published 2004 by Authentic Media
9 Holdom Avenue, Bletchley, Milton Keynes, MK1 1QR, UK
1820 Jet Stream Drive, Colorado Springs, CO 80921, USA
Medchal Road, Jeedimetla Village, Secunderabad 500 055, A.P., India
www.authenticmedia.co.uk

**Authentic Media is a division of IBS-STL U.K., limited by
guarantee, with its Registered Office at Kingstown Broadway,
Carlisle, Cumbria CA3 0HA. Registered in England & Wales No.
1216232. Registered charity 270162**

British Library Cataloguing in Publication Data

A catalogue record for this book is available
from the British Library

ISBN 978-1-85078-606-1

Printed and bound in the UK by J F Print Ltd, Sparkford, Somerset.

Cover design by 4-9-0 ltd
Print Management by Adare Carwin

Contents

Introduction

At a time when it is most needed, perhaps Lent is less popular within the Christian church than ever before. As the pace of life gets faster and the church struggles to keep up with constant change 'reflection' is becoming a thing of the past. But for many Lent is still a welcome spiritual retreat, an opportunity to take stock of our Christian lives. Lent refocuses us on the cross which points back to our sin and desperate need of a saviour and forwards to Christ's return and the urgency to prepare for heaven. Such reflection helps restore us, refreshing our hearts and renewing our vision to live out our faith.

The aim of this study guide is to help you in your spiritual journey this Lent. It is a compilation of chapters from books that have become much-loved classics in our time. Questions have been added to the end of each chapter to help you reflect and apply the timeless truths to your own situation.

You can use this book in your own personal devotions or as part of a group. If you are using the book as a Lenten study you probably won't have time to cover all the chapters so simply focus on the ones most relevant to the needs of your particular group.

1. Forgiveness

by Max Lucado

Fatal Errors

The handwriting was shaky. The stationery was lined loose-leaf paper. The ink was black and the tone desperate. The note was dated February 6, 1974 and was addressed to the U.S. government.

'I am sending ten dollars for blankets I stole while in World War II. My mind could not rest. Sorry I'm late.' It was signed, 'an ex-GI.' Then there was this postscript, 'I want to be ready to meet God.'

This recruit was not alone in his guilt. His letter is one of literally tons of letters that have been sent to the U.S. government since it began collecting and storing the letters in 1811. Since that time $3,500,000 has been deposited in what is called the Conscience Fund.

An average of $45,000 per year is received. The biggest year was 1950 in which $350,000 was collected.

One man writing from Brazil sent fifty dollars to cover the cost of two pairs of cavalry boots, two pairs of trousers, one case of rations and thirty pounds of frozen meat he stole from the army between 1943 and 1946.

In some instances the amounts are small, only the remorse is big. One Colorado woman sent in two eight-cent stamps to make up for having used one stamp twice (which for some reason had not been cancelled.) A former Inland Revenue employee sent in one dollar for four ballpoint pens she had never returned to the office.

A Salem, Ohio, man submitted one dollar with the following note, 'When a boy, I put a few pennies on the railroad track and the train flattened them. I also used a dime or a quarter in a silver-coating experiment in high school. I understand there is a law against defacing our money. I have not seen it but I desire to be a law-abiding citizen.'

Anxiety over a thirty-year-old mistake? Regret over squashed pennies? A guilty conscience because of ballpoint pens? If the struggle to have a clean conscience wasn't so common, the letters would be funny. But the struggle *is* common.

What do you do with your failures? Our mistakes come to us as pebbles; small stones that serve as souvenirs of our stumbles. We carry them in our hands, and soon our hands are full. We put them in our pockets, and soon our pockets bulge. We place them in a sack and put it over our shoulder; the jute scratches and chaps. And soon the bag of yesterday's failures is so heavy, we drag it.

Here are some failures that have been dragged into my office.

Unfaithfulness. He wanted to try again. She said, 'No Way.' He wanted a second chance. She said, 'You blew your chance.' He admitted that he made a mistake by seeing another woman. He sees now that the mistake was fatal to his marriage.

Homosexuality. His wrists bore the scars of a suicide attempt. His arms had tracks from countless needles. His eyes reflected the spirit of one hell-bent on self-destruction. His words were those of a prisoner grimly resigned to the judge's sentence. 'I'm gay. My dad says I'm a queer. I guess he's right.'

Division. A church leadership demanded submission. A membership demanded a louder voice. It was a bomb waiting to explode. The eruption resulted in a half-empty building of walking wounded.

Immorality. She came to church with a pregnant womb and repentant spirit. 'I can't have a child,' she pleaded. 'We'll find a home for it,' she was assured. She agreed. Then she changed her mind. Her boyfriend funded the abortion. 'Can God ever forgive me?' she asked.

Nothing drags more stubbornly than a sack of failures.

Could you do it all over again, you'd do it differently. You'd be a different person. You'd be more patient. You'd control your tongue. You'd finish what you started. You'd turn the other cheek instead of slapping his. You'd get married first. You wouldn't marry at all. You'd be honest. You'd resist the temptation. You'd run around with a different crowd.

But you can't. And as many times as you tell yourself, 'What's done is done,' what you did can't be undone.

That's part of what Paul meant when he said, 'The wages of sin is death' (Rom 6:23). He didn't say, 'The wages of sin is a bad mood.' Or, 'The wages of sin is a hard day.' Nor, 'The wages of sin is depression.' Read it again. 'The wages of sin is death.' Sin is fatal.

Can anything be done with it?

Your therapist tells you to talk about it. So you do. You pull the sack into his office and pour the rocks out on his floor and analyse each one. And it's helpful. It feels good to talk and he's nice. But when the hour is up, you still have to carry the sack out with you.

Your friends tell you not to feel bad. 'Everyone slumps a bit in this world,' they say. 'Not very comforting,' you say.

Feel-great-about-life rallies tell you to ignore the thing and be happy! Which works – until you wipe the mist off your mirror and take an honest look. Then you see, it's still there.

Legalists tell you to work the weight off. A candle for every rock. A prayer for every pebble. Sounds logical, but what if I run out of time? Or what if I didn't count correctly? You panic.

What *do* you do with the stones from life's stumbles?

My oldest daughter, Jenna, is four years old. Some time ago she came to me with a confession. 'Daddy, I took a crayon and drew on the wall.' (Kids amaze me with their honesty.)

I sat down and lifted her up into my lap and tried to be wise. 'Is that a good thing to do?' I asked her.

'No.'

'What does Daddy do when you write on the wall?'

'You spank me.'

'What do you think Daddy should do this time?'

'Love.'

Don't we all want that? Don't we all long for a father who, even though our mistakes are written all over the wall, will love us anyway? Don't we want a father who cares for us in spite of our failures?

We *do* have that type of a father. A father who is at his best when we are at our worst. A father whose grace is strongest when our devotion is weakest. If your bag is big and bulky, then you're in for some thrilling news: your failures are not fatal.

Cristo Redentor

Ninety feet tall. One thousand three hundred and twenty tons of reinforced Brazilian concrete. Positioned on a mountain a mile and a half above sea level. It's the famous *Christ the Redeemer* statue that overlooks the city of Rio de Janeiro, Brazil.

No tourist comes to Rio without snaking up Corcovado mountain to see this looming monument. The head alone is nine feet tall. The span from fingertip to fingertip – sixty-three feet.

While living in Rio, I saw the statue dozens of times. But no time was as impressive as the first.

I was a college student spending a summer in Brazil. Except for scampers across the Mexican border, this was my first trip outside the continental U.S. I had known this monument only through *National Geographic* magazine. I was to learn that no magazine can truly capture the splendour of *Cristo Redentor*.

Below me was Rio. Seven million people swarming on the lush green mountains that crash into the bright blue Atlantic. Behind me was the *Christ the Redeemer* statue. As I looked at the towering edifice through my telephoto lens, two ironies caught my attention.

I couldn't help but notice the blind eyes. Now, I know what you are thinking – all statues have blind eyes. You are right, they do. But it's as if the sculptor of this statue intended that the eyes be blind. There are no pupils to suggest vision. There are no circles to suggest sight. There are only Little Orphan Annie openings.

I lowered my camera to my waist. *What kind of redeemer is this? Blind? Eyes fixed on the horizon, refusing to see the mass of people at its feet?*

I saw the second irony as I again raised my camera. I followed the features downward; past the strong nose, past the prominent chin, past the neck. My focus came to rest on the cloak of the statue. On the outside of the cloak there is a heart. A Valentine's heart. A simple heart.

A stone heart.

The unintended symbolism staggered me. *What kind of redeemer is this? Heart made of stone? Held together, not with passion and love, but by concrete and mortar. What kind of redeemer is this? Blind eyes and stony heart?*

I've since learned the answer to my own question: What kind of redeemer is this? Exactly the kind of redeemer most people have.

Oh, most people would not admit to having a blind redeemer with a stone heart. But take a close look.

For some, Jesus is a good-luck charm. The 'Rabbit's Foot Redeemer'. Pocket-sized. Handy.

Easily packaged. Easily understood. Easily diagrammed. You can put his picture on your wall or you can stick it in your wallet as insurance. You can frame him. Dangle him from your rear-view mirror or glue him to your dashboard.

His speciality? Getting you out of a jam. Need a parking place? Rub the redeemer. Need help on a quiz? Pull out the rabbit's foot. No need to have a relationship with him. No need to love him. Just keep him in your pocket next to your four-leaf clover.

For many he's an 'Aladdin's Lamp Redeemer'. New jobs. New cars. New and improved spouses. Your wish is his command. And what's more, he conveniently re-enters the lamp when you don't want him around.

The 'Rabbit's Foot Redeemer'. The 'Aladdin's Lamp Redeemer'. Few demands, no challenges. No need for sacrifice. No need for commitment.

Sightless and heartless redeemers. Redeemers without power. That's not the Redeemer of the New Testament.

Compare the blind Christ I saw in Rio to the compassionate one seen by a frightened woman early one morning in Jerusalem (John 8:1–11).

It's dawn. The early morning sun stretches a golden blanket across the streets of the city. Diamonds of dew cling to blades of grass. A cat stretches as it awakens. The noises are scattered.

A cockerel crows his early morning recital.

A dog barks to welcome the day.

A peddler shuffles down the street, his wares on his back.

And a young carpenter speaks in the courtyard.

Jesus sits surrounded by a horseshoe of listeners. Some nod their heads in agreement and open their hearts in obedience. They have accepted the teacher as their teacher and are learning to accept him as their Lord.

Others are curious, wanting to believe yet wary of this one whose claims so stretch the boundaries of belief.

Whether cautious or convinced, they listen keenly. They arose early. There was something about his words that was more comforting than sleep.

We don't know his topic that morning. Prayer, perhaps. Or maybe kindness or anxiety. But whatever it was, it was soon interrupted when people burst into the courtyard

Determined, they erupt out of a narrow street and stomp towards Jesus. The listeners scramble to get out of the way. The mob is made up of religious leaders, the elders and deacons of their day. Respected and important men. And struggling to keep her balance on the crest of this angry wave is a scantily-clad woman.

Only moments before she had been in bed with a man who was not her husband. Was this how she made her living? Maybe. Maybe not. Maybe her husband was gone, her heart was lonely, the stranger's touch was warm, and before she knew it, she had done it. We don't know.

But we do know that a door was jerked open and she was yanked from a bed. She barely had time to cover her body before she was dragged into the street by two men the age of her father. What thoughts raced through her mind as she struggled to keep her feet?

Curious neighbours stuck heads through open windows. Sleepy dogs yelped at the rumpus.

And now, with bold strides, the mob storms towards the teacher. They throw the woman in his direction. She nearly falls.

'We found this woman in bed with a man!' cries the leader. 'The law says to stone her. What do you say?'

Cocky with borrowed courage, they smirk as they watch the mouse go for the cheese.

The woman searches the faces, hungry for a compassionate glance. She finds none. Instead, she sees accusation. Squinting eyes. Tight lips. Gritted teeth. Stares that sentence without seeing.

Cold, stony hearts that condemn without feeling.

She looks down and sees the rocks in their hands – the rocks of righteousness intended to stone the lust out of her. The men squeeze them so tightly that their fingertips are white. They squeeze them as if the rocks were the throat of this preacher they hate.

In her despair she looks at the Teacher. His eyes don't glare. 'Don't worry,' they whisper, 'it's okay.' And for the first time that morning she sees kindness.

When Jesus saw her, what did he see? Did he see her as a father sees his grown daughter as she walks down the wedding aisle? The father's mind races back through time watching his girl grow up again – from nappies to dolls. From classrooms to boyfriends. From the first date to the wedding day. The father sees it all as he looks at his daughter.

As Jesus looked at this daughter, did his mind race back? Did he relive the act of forming this child in heaven? Did he see her as he had originally made her?

'Knitted together' is how the psalmist described the process of God making man (Ps 139:13). Not manufactured or mass-produced, but knitted. Each thread of personality tenderly intertwined. Each string of temperament deliberately selected.

God as creator. Pensive. Excited. Inventive.

An artist, brush on pallet, seeking the perfect shade.

A composer, fingers on keyboard, listening for the exact chord.

A poet, pen poised on paper, awaiting the precise word.

The Creator, the master weaver, threading together the soul.

Each one different. No two alike. None identical.

On earth, Jesus was an artist in a gallery of his own paintings. He was a composer listening as the orchestra interpreted his music. He was a poet hearing his own poetry. Yet his works of art had been defaced. Creation after battered creation.

He had created people for splendour. They had settled for mediocrity. He had formed them with love. They had scarred each other with hate.

When he saw businessmen using God-given intelligence to feed Satan-given greed ...

When he saw tongues he had designed to encourage used as daggers to cut ...

When he saw hands that had been given for holding used as weapons for hurting ...

When he saw eyes into which he'd sprinkled joy now burning with hatred …

I wonder, did it weary him to see hearts that were stained, even discarded?

Jesus saw such a heart as he looked at this woman. Her feet were bare and muddy. Her arms hid her chest and her hands clutched each other under her chin. And her heart, her heart was ragged; torn as much by her own guilt as by the mob's anger.

So, with the tenderness only a father can have, he set out to untie the knots and repair the holes.

He begins by diverting the crowd's attention. He draws on the ground. Everybody looks down. The woman feels relief as the eyes of the men look away from her.

The accusers are persistent. 'Tell us teacher! What do you want us to do with her?'

He could have asked why they didn't bring the man. The Law indicted him as well. He could have asked why they were suddenly blowing the dust off an old command that had sat on the shelves for centuries. But he didn't.

He just raised his head and offered an invitation, 'I guess if you've never made a mistake, then you have a right to stone this woman.' He looked back down and began to draw on the earth again.

Someone cleared his throat as if to speak, but no one spoke. Feet shuffled. Eyes dropped. Then thud … thud … thud … rocks fell to the ground.

And they walked away. Beginning with the greyest beard and ending with the blackest, they turned and left. They came as one, but they left one by one.

Jesus told the woman to look up. 'Is there no one to condemn you?' He smiled as she raised her head. She saw no one, only rocks – each one a miniature tombstone to mark the burial place of a man's arrogance.

'Is there no one to condemn you?' he'd asked. *There is still one who can,* she thinks. And she turns to look at him. *What does he want? What will he do?*

Maybe she expected him to scold her. Perhaps she expected him to walk away from her. I'm not sure, but I do know this: what she got, she never expected. She got a promise and a commission.

The promise: 'Then neither do I condemn you.'

The commission: 'Go and sin no more.'

The woman turns and walks away into anonymity.

She's never seen or heard from again. But we can be confident of one thing: on that morning in Jerusalem, she saw Jesus and Jesus saw her. And could we somehow transport her to Rio de Janeiro and let her stand at the base of the *Cristo Redentor,* I know what her response would be.

'That's not the Jesus I saw,' she would say. And she would be right. For the Jesus she saw didn't have a hard heart. And the Jesus that saw her didn't have blind eyes.

However, if we could somehow transport her to Calvary and let her stand at the base of the cross ... you know what she would say. 'That's him,' she would whisper. 'That's him.'

She would recognize his hands. The only hands that had held no stones that day were his. And on this day they still hold no stones. She would recognize his voice. It's raspier and weaker, but the words are the same, 'Father, forgive them. ...' And she would recognize his eyes. How could she ever forget those eyes? Clear and tear-filled. Eyes that saw her not as she was, but as she was intended to be.

Study Questions

1 *Reflect on the author's portrayal of Jesus as a Father, Redeemer and Creator. What aspect of these descriptions means the most to you?*

2 *Discuss the reasons why people, both Christians and non-Christians, find it difficult to accept God's forgiveness? Why do we look to other people and other means to clear our consciences?*

3 *Consider Lucado's description of the woman caught in adultery. What difference did God's forgiveness make to her? If we fully appreciated God's forgiveness what difference would it make to our lives?*

4 *Reread John 8:1-11 together. As you consider your own personal struggle to forgive certain individuals what does this passage teach you?*

5 *If Jesus, with his seeing eyes and compassionate heart, visited your area what would he say/do to you, to the others in your small group, to the people in your community? What priorities of his do we need to learn to share? How can we do this during the season of Lent?*

2. 'Onl

by Eve

Wow! I stopped for a se
Do I insult these people b
will? What do I do abo
in-law and brothe
have done? I
teach the
Whe
Chr
14

'This is the assurance we have in approaching God: that if we ask anything according to his will, he hears us. And if we know that he hears us – whatever we ask – we know that we have what we asked of him.'
1 John 5:14-15

On the morning following Lindon Karo's funeral, I posed some searching questions to those attending our prayer meeting. 'What do you think went wrong? Why did this tremendous minister, only thirty-two years old, die of cancer? Thousands of prayers were offered for him. Forty people in his church had promised to fast and pray one day a week for him. I don't think I attended a meeting anywhere during that period, but that we were all praying. Why weren't those prayers answered? What went wrong? Why did we bury Lindon Karo yesterday?'

When I reached this point in the meeting, a committee member (wanting to be helpful) waved her hand from the back of the church, and said, 'Yes, Evelyn, and Lindon Karo's mother-in-law and sister-in-law are here with us today.'

...ond and pondered, *Do I go on?*
... teaching about how to pray in God's
...ut these loved ones who buried their son-
...-in-law just yesterday? What would you
...elt God was telling me to go ahead and
...esson.

...n the session was over, those two very beautiful
...stian women came to me and said, 'Please don't
worry about today's talk. Many months ago we as a
family committed the whole matter of Lindon's illness to
the Lord. We prayed, "Only Your will, God, whatever it
is." We did not ask for healing only; we prayed that God's
will be done in our loved one's life.'

Have you come to the place where you can pray, 'Only
God's will'? Do you know that you are in absolute
oneness with the will of God? Have you come to that
place?

We read in 1 John 5:14-15 about a prerequisite to
effective praying.

> *This is the assurance we have in approaching God: that if we ask*
> *anything according to his will, he hears us. And if we know that*
> *he hears us – whatever we ask – we know that we have what we*
> *asked of him.* 1 John 5:14-15

Did you catch the prerequisite? How can we have
confidence in anything we ask? It is by praying *according
to His will*. And what is confidence in prayer? It is
knowing absolutely and assuredly that we have
whatever we have asked.

'If it be Your will, Amen'

What do we mean when we use the expression 'praying
in God's will'? Is it simply tacking on the end of prayer

the phrase we use perhaps more frequently than any other? You know how it goes. We ask God for a whole string of things, then we piously add, '… if it be Your will, Lord. Amen.' Or it may be that we ask God for something we know is not good for us. Let's say, for example, that we ask for a crate of Mars bars! God knows very well (and so do we) that if we ate a crate of Mars bars we'd die of indigestion, but many times we ask Him for something just as ridiculous and tack on 'if it be Your will,' just to get ourselves off the hook. This is not what it means to pray in God's will.

The praying person

The New Testament Greek tutor in a nearby college, said to me one day, 'Evelyn, I hope that when you're teaching all those women to pray in God's will that you are teaching them that it is the person praying, and not the prayer request, that changes.'

I said, 'That's the whole emphasis of our lesson on God's will.'

Praying in God's will is not easy, yet it's very simple. It involves a commitment of every single thing that comes into our lives to God and His perfect will. And it's exciting to live in complete oneness with the will of God. It is never dull or static because it is not a one-time, once-for-all commitment. It is something we have to work at constantly, moment by moment.

This is expressed in a beautiful definition of the word 'effective' as it is found in James 5:16. According to Vine's *Expository Dictionary of New Testament Words*, it means 'the effect produced in the praying person, bringing him into line with the will of God.' It is the person who changes, rather than the prayer. Praying 'in the will of

God' then means being conformed to the will of God as we pray. Wouldn't it be great if we could always *be conformed to the will of God* (with all known sin confessed), so that we would never pray outside the will of God? The effective prayer person, then, is one who is completely committed to God's will for answers, and not to his own will.

After our women had been praying for a few months back in 1968, my husband exclaimed one day, 'Even if God doesn't answer a single one of your prayers, what He's doing in the people who are praying will be worth it all.'

What God does in the lives of people who are praying, in bringing them in line with His will, is one of His miracles here in this world. The turning point in our prayer meetings is the session where people in prayer commit their whole lives to God's perfect will. This happened to a school teacher, who sent me this note recently:

> On February 26 my sister invited me to attend your prayer meeting. I thought, *A prayer meeting? What good will it do? I have prayed and prayed, and it hasn't done any good.* But I went. You see, I have been a Christian all my life. I had a wonderful Christian home and brought up in an atmosphere of loving and trusting Jesus. But, suddenly, I was faced with very severe testing of my faith. My husband's building firm collapsed, leaving a large debt for which we were half responsible. Because of this, we had to sell our home and sell everything. Also, I was not well, and our little two-year-old son had just had an operation.
>
> Then, the passage that was to change my life and my prayers, 1 John 5:14-15, "and this is the assurance...". Up to that point I had not prayed for His will. I could only see what I wanted to happen.

At the end of the session Evelyn asked us to stand and form our prayer groups of four. She told us to ask God for the *one* thing we wanted most from Him. I remember saying aloud in my little circle of four Christian sisters, "Lord, I want Your perfect will for me and my family."

That was it! I was to learn later that was what was keeping my prayers from being answered. I had never asked God for His will.

Now, I feel entirely free. I felt the whole load lift, as if the responsibility to straighten up the messy things was not mine.

Now it is nine months since that time, and I cannot begin to tell you of the peace I have in my heart. My husband's business debts are not all cleared up as yet, but God is moving. The burden is lifted. My health has improved tremendously. In fact, I got a teaching position at Bible college this autumn, a position that just seemed to come right out of heaven itself. I was not applying or seeking such a position, but was asked to join the staff. Praise God! He can "do immeasurably more than all we ask or imagine" (Eph 3:20).

On earth, as in heaven

For us to pray, 'Lord, I want Your will down here on earth,' is a tremendous prayer. Wouldn't it be fantastic if we could pray that prayer for London today? If we could by our praying get God's will done in the USA or Moscow, or in the Middle East? While there is a sense in which we can pray that God's will be done in these places, they are not within our direct sphere of influence, are they? But there is a spot on earth, a sphere of influence that belongs only to you. It has been given to you by our heavenly Father. And it's possible for you to bring about God's complete will in your sphere of influence here on earth.

The disciples whom Jesus taught to pray, 'Our Father...Your will be done on earth as in heaven', knew they couldn't change the whole Roman Empire, but they also knew it was possible for them to change the spheres of influence which were theirs, which had been given to them by God. And they did. God changes circumstances and people when we in a very personal way pray that His will be done in the sphere of influence which is ours.

The Lord's Prayer really comes into focus right where we are when we pray, 'Your will be done on earth as in heaven.' Is there anything contrary to God's will in heaven? No! Think of what would happen if every Christian really brought God's will to the little sphere that is his, with nothing contrary to God's perfect will! How different would be our nation, our cities, our churches, our homes.

The example of Christ

The supreme example of praying in the will of God is that of Christ praying in the garden of Gethsemane on the night before He was to die on the cross for our sins. Our Lord, in His humanity, did not want to suffer. He prayed, 'Father, if You are willing, take this cup from me; yet not my will, but Yours be done' (Luke 22:42). Then, after much agony of spirit, He said: 'Father, I am willing for Your will.'

Have you come to the place in your life where you can say, 'Lord, not my will, but Yours be done? No matter how much it hurts, how difficult the task, how high the mountain You've given me to climb, it doesn't make any difference, dear Lord, I am willing'?

When we visited the Holy Land a few years ago, I sat alone under one of those old, gnarled olive trees in the garden of Gethsemane, and read in Luke's Gospel the account of all my Jesus went through the night before He died, before He took upon Himself the sin of the world, including mine; when He sweated as it were great drops of blood there in the garden. With my heart absolutely breaking, I wrote in the margin of my Bible, 'Lord, please, only Your will in my life, only Your will!' We don't have to sit under an ancient olive tree in His land to come to that place, but right where we are today we can say to Christ, 'Lord, not my will, only Yours be done.'

When we reach the place where we're really on our faces before God, does He as an 'ogre' sitting up in heaven say, 'Good, I have another doormat on which to wipe My feet'? Is that what He says? Do we become doormats for God to wipe His feet on when we say, 'Lord, I'm willing for Your will'? Oh, no. What happened to Christ the day after He said this to His heavenly Father? He became the *Redeemer of mankind!* He became your Saviour and my Saviour.

Mary, too, had a tremendous privilege because she was willing for God's will in her life. Do you recall her response at the time of the Annunciation? When the angel came to her and said that God had chosen her to be the mother of the Saviour, Mary immediately responded, 'I am the Lord's servant. May it be to me as you have said'.

Do you think it was easy for Mary to say yes to the will of God, to being pregnant out of wedlock? When it meant vulnerability to misunderstanding, to ridicule? When it could mean possible rejection by her fiance or even being stoned to death? It was not easy for Mary, but because she was willing for God's will, she was greatly blessed by Him. She was given the great privilege of bearing the Son who became our Redeemer.

Open doors

What happens to Evelyn when she is on her face before God and says, 'OK, Lord, I don't know what You want. That's a big mountain, that's difficult surgery, these are hard things in my life, but, Lord, no matter what it is, I want Your perfect will'? At that point does God become an ogre and take advantage of my commitment? No, at that point He starts to open doors, and fantastic things begin to happen – even prayer conferences when I just make myself available to Him.

One day our college chaplain inquired, 'Eve, how did you ever get all those prayer meetings started, anyway?' I shrugged, 'They just sort of grew, like Topsy.' He looked at me, wondering at what I was saying. I went on, 'You know, we really didn't plan them. They just happened. In every single step, the constant prayer of local committees, prayer chains, and our general committee has been, "Lord, Your will." Then we wait to see what His will is. We never even make contacts asking to hold a course, and it is so thrilling to watch God work when we let Him.'

One day a young woman who had travelled almost one hundred miles round trip each day to attend a Minneapolis prayer conference asked me, 'What is the procedure to get you to come to our town for a prayer conference?' I replied, 'Pray about it, and if it is God's will we'll come.' 'Oh, three of us have been praying for several months,' she replied, 'and we believe God is saying we should have it.'

'That's good enough for me,' I said. 'I'll come.' I better understood her insistence on having a conference in her town when she handed me this note:

Dear Evelyn: since being in your prayer conferences my life has been changed through accepting Christ. Also, my four-year-old daughter and nine-year-old son have asked Jesus into their lives. Now my husband wants me to work on him. Thank you.

God rewarded her eagerness when thirty women found Christ in 'her' conference. It was God's will! In fact, the inter-church Bible study on prayer, that automatically turned into our first prayer conference, came into being because God took over. The chairman and I, frustrated at not being able to work my schedule into all the autumn events of that area, finally in tears just prayed together, 'All right, Lord, only *Your* will. Whenever *You* want this Bible study, let it work out.' And God timed it perfectly. He knew all along when prayer would be needed in that town. He knew that the next February, witches and occult personnel would be in one of the high schools, so He planned for those two hundred and fifty women to be 'praying together' just at the right time.

What has turned into this whole prayer ministry in my life started in November 1967, when I was asked by my denomination to work with women in our church and discover what happened when women prayed. I hesitated at first, not knowing for certain whether to make the commitment. But one day while I was reading God's Word, a phrase in Revelation, 'See, I have placed before you an open door,' stood out as if it were in bold print. God said, 'Evelyn, I have placed before *you* an open door.' I closed my Bible, said, 'Lord, I'm willing,' and went to make a long distance phone call. I said excitedly to the secretary of our National Women's committee, 'How can I say no when God has just put before me an open door in Revelation 3:8?'

Has God put before you an open door? Are you hesitating, perhaps rebelling, or holding back because of fear, when God is challenging, 'Look, here's an open door, wouldn't you like to walk through it for Me? This is My will for you.'

Oh, answer Him, 'Lord, here I am. There is no friction between my will and Yours. Whatever You have for me, I know that You will give me enough strength, enough grace. I know You will give me all that I need, so Lord here I am ready to do Your will.'

'Try it. You'll like it!' It's amazing what happens when we step out.

Men too?

Sometimes I seem to need a little help from other people in going through the doors God is opening for me. 'I don't think God is keen for you to teach men to pray, but I think you are,' a full-time church worker chided as we chatted at a Christmas party. I suddenly realized that I was so sold on the idea that I was praying, 'God, Your will,' but didn't have the courage to accept it.

My prayer-chains had been praying for several months about frequent requests for me to attend prayer meetings. Then I learned that, while I was planning to give a three-minute speech the next Sunday encouraging attendance at our up-coming meeting, the host church was planning for me to give *the* morning talk. I was panicking, just *knowing* it never could be God's will for me to do *that!*

Suddenly, as we were together praying, a prayer-chain member prayed, 'Lord, we're sick and tired of praying this request. We're going to test it. The way the men accept Evelyn next Sunday morning will be our answer as to whether she opens the prayer meetings to men or not.' I nearly fainted as she prayed. *I* never would have dared talk to God like that.

The next Saturday I received a call from a woman in one of St. Paul's suburbs. 'I've met with some of our leaders (we're without a minister at present), and we want an evening prayer meeting in our church that is open to men, women, and young people. We definitely feel it is God's will.' 'I'll give you my answer on Monday,' I stalled, not daring to tell her I had to see how the 'test' came out the next day! With fear and trembling I shared 'What Happens When We Pray' with that Sunday congregation. After the service the knuckles of my right hand were white from all those men shaking hands and thanking me. Nine days later we started our first prayer meeting for women *and men.* Sometimes I need a little pushing to go through doors God is opening. Do you?

If you want me, Lord

One Friday afternoon during our first prayer meetings, I asked my small telephone prayer-chain of ten members to pray that God would keep my schedule in balance speaking against the occult and on prayer. That night, in one of those deep devotional times that come periodically in many of our lives, I prayed, 'Lord, I don't know what it is, but I want Your will, just Your will.' And I meant it. Then, out of the blue it seemed (but I'm sure it was God-inspired), I heard myself promising God that I would be involved in two areas if He wanted me to. One was the Billy Graham Crusade which was due to be held that coming summer; the other was a national women's prayer movement.

The very next morning my telephone rang. It was Myrl Glockner. She said, 'Evelyn, we've never met, but I just felt I had to call and ask you if you will be one of eleven committee members to get 5,000 prayer groups going for the Billy Graham Crusade.

Do you want time to pray about it?'

I was stunned, 'Myrl,' I stammered, 'I don't need time to pray. How can I say no when just last night I said so completely, "Lord, Your will, if You want me to be involved in the Billy Graham Crusade."'

On the following Tuesday, after I had completed a session on prayer, a woman came down the aisle of the church waving a paper and calling, 'Evelyn, I have a message here for you from Vonette Bright of the Prayer Crusade. She would like you to become involved in the programme.'

Friday, Saturday, and Tuesday. There it was – God's opening of two doors when I told Him I was willing for His will for me with those two organizations. It's a very exciting thing. Don't say, 'I want it my way, Lord,' but 'Lord, Your way. Whatever You have for me, I'm Yours. Just take me, open any door, lead me in that direction.' You will be astounded at what God will do. You will be out of breath trying to keep up with the opportunities. Phone calls will come from people you didn't even know existed. Who inspired that person to call and ask you to go here or there to minister? Nobody – but God.

For You to Pray

'*O God, I want only Your will in my life. Open the doors You have for me, and give me the courage and faith to go through them.*'

Study questions

1 *What has encouraged or challenged you most from this chapter?*
2 *Share together examples of when you have specifically prayed 'Lord not my will, but Yours be done'. If it is*

appropriate explain the situation, how God worked in it, and how you responded.

3   Before we can pray for God's will to be done in our lives we need to confess our sins. What are the sins of the 21st century? What does the church and we as Christians need to repent of?

4   If it is appropriate, share in twos what ambitions, plans, attitudes or relationships you need to set aside so that you can pray with honesty, 'Lord, not my will, but Yours be done.'

5   Spend time looking at these prayers from the Bible. What do they teach us about how and what to pray?
*   Genesis 18:20–33
*   1 Samuel 2:1–10
*   Ezra 9:5–15
*   Psalm 51

6   Evelyn Christenson talks about spheres of influence. What people, institutions, or events are in your particular sphere of influence? How can you pray for them, how can you promote God's will in these areas?

3. Holy Sacrifice

by Elisabeth Elliot

A TELEVISION COMMERCIAL shows a man springing out of bed, racing down the stairs, gulping a cup of coffee, snatching up coat and briefcase, and exploding out the front door. The message: 'The day can't begin soon enough for a man compelled by a single aim in life.' He's a Bache broker. He can't wait to get to the office to find out what's happening on the market, but grabs the kitchen phone and asks, 'How did we open in London today?'

The lust for money and power moves men when a bulldozer wouldn't move them otherwise. They will punish their bodies, spending most of their waking hours sitting in an office chair, then working out furiously in a gymnasium or on a jogging track, eating tiny breakfasts, tremendous 'business' lunches, and high-calorie dinners, all in order to get ahead in the world and enjoy some of its pleasures for a season.

Holiness has never been the driving force of the majority. It is, however, mandatory for anyone who wants to enter the Kingdom. 'Aim at ... a holy life, for without that no one will see the Lord.'

'For you know what orders we gave you, in the name of the Lord Jesus,' wrote Paul to the Thessalonians. 'This is the will of God, that you should be holy: you must abstain from fornication; each one of you must learn to gain mastery over his body, to hallow and honour it, not giving way to lust like the pagans who are ignorant of God ... For God called us to holiness, not to impurity.'

Discipline, for a Christian, begins with the body. We have only one. It is this body that is the primary material given to us for sacrifice. If we didn't have this, we wouldn't have anything. We are meant to present it, offer it up, give it unconditionally to God for His purposes. This, we are told, is an 'act of spiritual worship.' The giving of this physical body, comprising blood, bone, and tissue, worth a few dollars in chemicals, becomes a spiritual act, 'for such is the worship which you, as rational creatures, should offer.'

The Jerusalem Bible translates it this way: 'Think of God's mercy, my brothers, and worship Him, I beg you, in a way that is worthy of thinking beings,' [that is, a note tells us, " 'in a spiritual way,' as opposed to the ritual sacrifices of Jews or pagans"] 'by offering your living bodies as a holy sacrifice...'

More spiritual failure is due, I believe, to this cause than to any other: the failure to recognize this living body as having anything to do with worship or holy sacrifice. This body is, quite simply, the starting place. Failure here is failure everywhere else.

'He who would see the face of the most powerful Wrestler, our boundless God,' wrote Arozco, 'must first have wrestled with himself.'

Only one who has taken seriously the correlation between the physical and spiritual and begun the struggle can appreciate the aptness of that word *wrestle*. Habits, for example, hold a half nelson on us. That hold must be broken if we are to be free for the Lord's service. We cannot give our hearts to God and keep our bodies for ourselves.

What sort of body is this?

It's mortal. It will not last. It was made of dust to begin with and after death will return to dust. Paul called it a 'vile' body, or one 'belonging to our humble state,' a 'body of sin,' a 'dead' body because of sin. But it is also a temple or shrine for the Holy Spirit; it is a 'member' of Christ's body. It is, furthermore – and this makes all the difference in how we should treat it – wholly redeemable, transfigurable, 'resurrectible.'

The Christian's body houses not only the Holy Spirit Himself, but the Christian's heart, will, mind, and emotions – all that plays a part in our knowing God and living for Him.

In my case, the 'house' is tall; it is Anglo-Saxon, middle-aged, and female. I was not asked about my preferences in any of these factors, but I was given a choice about the use I make of them. In other words, the body was a gift to me. Whether I will thank God for it and offer it as a holy sacrifice is for me to decide.

What is meant by disciplining the body?

A body needs food. Food is a question of discipline for us who live in very rich, very civilized, very self-indulgent countries. For those who have not the vast array of choices we have, food is a fundamental matter of subsistence and not a major hindrance to holiness.

Discipline is evident on every page of the life of Daniel. The story starts with his being chosen as one of a group of young men from noble and royal families in Israel to serve in the palace of Nebuchadnezzar, king of Babylon. The first thing that sets Daniel apart from the others is his decision not to eat the rich food provided for them by the royal household, but only vegetables and water. He did not want to be defiled. It must have been God who put the idea into Daniel's head. It was certainly God who made the master show kindness and goodwill toward Daniel by granting his request. It was the beginning of the Lord's preparation of a man whose spiritual fiber would be rigorously tested later on.

It is significant that only 10 percent of our nation's top executives are overweight. This seems to me to indicate that few men who have not succeeded in curbing the appetite will make it to the top. Physical restraint is basic to power. They do it for power in this world. We do it for power in another.

Christians ought to watch what they eat. I do not refer here only to overeating, which is a bad thing, but to eating the wrong things. Too many sweets, too many rich things, too much junk. Take a walk through any supermarket and note the space given to soft drinks, candy, packaged snack foods, dry cereals. We could do very well without any of these. Try it for a week. You may be surprised at how dependent you are on them. You might even discover that you are an addict.

As a missionary I lived most of the time in fairly remote regions of the South American jungle, where the food that was available was all 'natural.' We ate a lot of manioc, a starchy tuber cultivated by the Indians, which provided their 'staff of life.' We ate rice, beans, pineapples, papayas, eggs, and whatever meat might be available from time to time, which was not often. There were no prepared foods to fall back on. No between-meal snacks. We had sugar, brought in from the outside, which we used to make lemonade wherever lemons were grown. We also imported oatmeal, powdered milk, salt, flour, and sometimes luxuries like cheese and chocolate. But menus were relatively simple, and our health was always excellent. It is a good thing, it seems to me, to learn to do with less.

One way to begin to see how vastly indulgent we usually are is to fast.

Fasting was prescribed by Jewish law and has always been a part of Christian practice.

A friend of mine recounted how she had been hammering away at heaven's door for the answer to a certain prayer. Nothing seemed to be happening. She began to get angry at God because He wasn't doing anything. Then He seemed to say quietly, 'Why don't you fast?'

'Then it came over me,' she said. 'I didn't really *care* that much.'

Another friend said she disagreed thoroughly with the notion of fasting, because it was nothing more than an attempt to 'twist God's arm.' 'He knows what I need, and if He wants to give it to me, He can. There's no need to become an ascetic.'

There is little understanding today of the real purpose of hermits and anchorites. While there were undoubtedly some who thought to buy their way to heaven by crucifying the flesh, the true effectiveness was based on their willingness to serve by giving themselves wholly to prayer and contemplation. This involves sacrifice of one kind or another, today as yesterday. Hermits and anchorites chose solitude, poverty, withdrawal from the world, fasting. In some of the churches of England there still exist anchorages – cells in which anchorites were walled up for life. One such can still be seen at Chester-le-Street Parish Church, in the north of England. Food was passed to him; sometimes people spoke to him through an aperture; and he had a 'squint,' a slit in the wall through which he could observe mass in the church. The people of the town rejoiced to know that someone was always at prayer.

I know Christians who fast on a regular basis – one day a week, one meal a week, one meal a month, or on certain days of the church calendar. I know others who have found it very helpful to fast when they have some special matter for prayer – a difficult decision to make, a new project to begin, a sick friend they want to help.

In Antioch God told the disciples, while they were fasting, to set apart Barnabas and Saul. Then, '... after further fasting and prayer ... ,' they laid their hands on them and sent them off to do the work to which God had specially called them. In Lystra, Iconium, and Antioch, Paul appointed elders and then '... with prayer and fasting committed them to the Lord in whom they had put their faith.'

Bishop John Allen has given five good reasons to fast:

1. It helps us to identify with the hungry, whom we are commanded to serve
2. It reminds us to pray
3. It makes us open to God's call
4. It prompts us to reflect on the outworking of His call
5. It is a mysterious instrument of the Holy Spirit's work

There are some things fasting does not do. It has never helped me to forget about eating. In fact, I find myself thinking a great deal about it. (Perhaps I do not fast long enough.) It is a long day that is not broken by the usual three meals. One finds out what an astonishing amount of time is spent in the planning, purchasing, preparing, eating, and cleaning up of meals. The social aspect of fasting is perhaps the most awkward thing about it. Jesus told us not to let people know we are fasting, but to groom ourselves as usual so that only our Father, '...who is in the secret place...' will see. Sometimes it is quite impossible to keep one's fast a secret. I know one mother of a large family who fasts one day a week, but continues to cook for her family and sits down with them at the table to have a cup of clear tea. Her family is used to this, and does not mind. Some families might. God knows the individual's circumstances and the purpose of the heart. In Daniel's case God made it possible for him to carry out his desire.

Fasting will not necessarily enable you to concentrate. It is important not to become agitated with yourself if your mind wanders. Ask the Lord to help you to concentrate on prayer, Bible reading, meditation. When feelings of spiritual pride are detected, confess them. When the phone rings, answer it if you must. When thoughts of next week's meeting intrude, mention them also to God and leave them with Him while you go back to the business of your prayers. Don't be shocked at your own inability to 'be spiritual.' The greatest saints knew their sinfulness and their weaknesses.

> They who fain would serve Him best
> Are conscious most of wrong within.

Don't try to sit or kneel in one position for too long. Stand up to pray, walk around, go outdoors and pray as you walk. If it is not possible to pray aloud without attracting attention, pray in a whisper. That will be better for most of us than trying to pray only mentally, a method that often encourages little more than wool-gathering.

In ancient Jewish times a stubborn son who was a glutton and a drunkard was stoned to death.

Gluttony, one of the more obvious modern sins, is generally tacitly accepted. Little is said about it from the pulpit. It is too embarrassing; it gets down too close to where the people, often including the preacher, live. No one who is fat dares to preach about it – he has no room to talk. Seldom will one who is not fat have the courage to broach the subject, for he will be told he has no business to talk since he has never 'had a weight problem.' (How does anyone know? Maybe he practices what he preaches.) Who then is left to talk?

While a very small percentage of people are over-weight for physiological reasons, the vast majority simply eat too much of the wrong things. That's the long and the short of it. Calories that are not burned up are stored in fat.

Jean Nidetch, who founded Weight Watchers, said that she did not start solving her problem until she was willing to name it: FAT. She posted little signs all over the house – on mirrors, on the refrigerator, over the sink – FAT, FAT, FAT.

I once wrote an article about a boat trip in which I de-scribed one of my fellow passengers as a fat lady. It seems I touched a very sensitive nerve. Seldom do I hear from readers, but I am still getting angry letters about that article. All are from females, several of whom have been careful to explain that they themselves are not fat. 'But,' wrote one, 'I have some chunky friends.' I wondered if the friends would appreciate being called 'chunky.' The Bible says Eglon was a very fat man. Isn't it all right to write about a fat lady? If we see ourselves in her and are offended, it's time to do something about it.

Many a Christian has found the hardly hoped-for strength of the Lord when bringing to Him some very real, very difficult physical need. If weight has quite literally become a 'burden,' why should we not bring it to the Lord and ask for His help in overcoming it? Can my will not cooperate with His in this matter as in spiritual matters? For some, fasting might be the place where discipline begins, even if they are not overweight. For others, dieting will be the place, whether it means eliminating junk foods for the sake of sounder health or eliminating calories for the sake of a normal weight.

'You do not belong to yourselves. You were bought at a price. Then honour God in your body.'

Sleep is another necessity. It takes discipline to go to bed when you ought to, and it takes discipline to get up. Think about your habits. Be honest to God about them, and if you know they are not in line with a disciplined life, pray for His help and start doing something.

My father had a ready answer for those who expressed incredulity at his 'ability' to get up so early in the morning: 'You have to start the night before.'

My great Bible teacher, L. E. Maxwell, was asked by a friend how in the world he had ever 'gotten victory' that enabled him to rise at four or five. 'How long did it take? Did you have someone pray with you about it?'

'No, I get up,' was his reply.

We make a huge joke about our self-indulgence and treat with amusement our failure to pull ourselves out of bed early enough to get to work without a hectic rush. An eighteenth-century hymn by Thomas Ken would seem quaint nowadays:

Awake my soul, and with the sun
Thy daily stage of duty run:
Shake off dull sloth and joyful rise
To pay thy morning sacrifice.

Most of us do not very easily shake off dull sloth. '*Joyful* rise'? Not very realistic, is it? It does not come naturally for us. But it never did for anybody. We forget that. Dull sloth is natural. Human beings haven't changed much in the whole of human history. So instead of dismissing the hymn writer as hopelessly outdated, might we not ask God for His help in being joyful makers of sacrifice?

'I am my body's sternest master ...,' Paul said. He put this in the context of athletic contests for which the prize is a crown of fading leaves, but reminded the Corinthians that they were in a different kind of competition – for an eternal crown that cannot fade.

The body needs exercise. 'The training of the body does bring limited benefits. ...'

Pope John Paul praised athletics as a lesson in dealing with life:

> Every type of sport carries within itself a rich patrimony of values, which must be always kept present in order to be realized.
>
> The training in reflection, the proper commitment of one's own energies, the education of will, the control of sensitivity, the methodical preparation, perseverance, resistance, the endurance of fatigue and wounds, the domination of one's own faculties, the sense of joy, acceptance of rules, the spirit of renunciation and solidarity, loyalty to commitment, generosity towards the winners, serenity in defeat, patience towards all – these are a complex of moral realities which demand a true asceticism and validly contribute to forming the human being and the Christian.

In spite of the enormous popularity of organized and professional games, as well as of tennis and golf, I suppose that the overwhelming majority of people over twenty-one do not play anything, at least regularly.

Jogging and other forms of violent individual exercise may be suitable for some. For others they would be extreme. The important thing is to move around somehow. Don't ride when you can walk, and walk briskly. When you can climb stairs instead of taking an elevator, climb them. When you do housework, move quickly. If your life's work requires sitting at a desk most of the day, you will have to arrange to get your body into motion. One very neat device for people who find it hard to get outdoor exercise is a small trampoline, about four feet in diameter, which is low enough to fit under a bed when not in use and on which you can 'jog' without the risk of shinsplints or injuries to the joints. A doctor friend gave us one of these as a wedding gift – hoping, I suspect, that if Lars exercised, he might last longer than my other husbands.

The bodies we are given are sexual bodies, equipped for sexual intercourse. Modern advertising never lets us forget this. Popular songs refer to very little else. The fashion business thrives on sexual provocation through dress. But being sexually equipped is not a license for us to use the equipment in any way we choose. Like every other good gift that comes down from the Father of lights, the gift of sexual activity is meant to be used as He intended, within the clearly defined limits of His purpose, which is marriage. If marriage is not included in God's will for an individual, then sexual activity is not included either.

'What am I supposed to do, then, with all this? I've got so much to give – what if nobody takes it?'

Give it to God.

'But you cannot say that our physical body was made for sexual promiscuity; it was made for God, and God is the Answer to our deepest longings,' Paul wrote.

To offer my body to the Lord as a living sacrifice includes offering to Him my sexuality and all that that entails, even my unfulfilled longings.

Today this advice will be laughed out of court by most. Sexual control is regarded as a hang-up from which the truly mature have been liberated. There are those still, however – as there have been in every age – who hold as holy the intimate relationship between a man and a woman, recognizing in it a type of Christ's love for His own bride, His church. As such it is not to be profaned.

This attitude can be held only by the mind's being captive to Christ. It is a miracle of grace. Let us not imagine it is anything less.

Malcolm Muggeridge notes in his diary that Tolstoy 'tried to achieve virtue, and particularly continence, through the exercise of his will; St. Augustine saw that, for Man, there is no virtue without a miracle. Thus St. Augustine's asceticism brought him serenity, and Tolstoy's anguish, conflict, and the final collapse of his life into tragic buffoonery.'

This body, remember, is to be resurrected. As John Donne pointed out long ago, the immortality of the soul is acceptable to man's natural reason, but the resurrection of the body must be a matter of faith.

> Where are all the atoms of the flesh which corrosion or consumption has eaten away? In what furrow or bowl of the earth lie all the ashes of a body burned a thousand years since? In what comer of the sea lies all the jelly of a body drowned in the general flood? What coherence, what sympathy, what dependence maintain any relation or correspondence between that arm that was lost in Europe and that leg that was lost in Africa or Asia with scores of years between?
>
> One humor of our dead body produces worms and those worms exhaust all other humor and then all dies and dries and molders into dust, and that dust is blown into the river and that water tumbles into the sea, which ebbs and flows in infinite revolutions.
>
> Still, God knows in what cabinet every seed pearl lies and in what part of the world every grain of every man's dust lies, and (as His prophet speaks in another case) He beckons for the bodies of His saints, and in the twinkling of an eye

that body that was scattered over all the elements has sat
down at the right of God in a glorious resurrection.

The knowledge that his body will one day be '... sown as
an animal body... raised as a spiritual body' ought to give
a disciple pause, ought to spur him to think of the use he
makes of it in this world. Even though flesh and blood
can never possess the Kingdom, think of its particles
being 'beckoned' to sit down with the Lord some day.

1   *What particular quote, illustration, line of argument or
    thought impacted you most from this chapter?*
2   *Elisabeth Elliot says 'this body was a gift to me.' How does
    secular society view the body? In what ways does this
    contrast with the Christian worldview?*
3   *Why do you think the church has failed to promote the
    discipline of the body? What priority do you think this
    particular discipline should be given in our lives?*
4   *Is fasting 'twisting God's arm' or 'a mysterious instrument
    of the Holy Spirit's work'? How do the following Bible
    references help you understand the place of fasting in a
    believer's life? Deuteronomy 9:18-21, 2 Samuel 12:15-20,
    Ezra 10:5-6, Esther 4:15-16, Jonah 3:7-10, Matthew 6:16-
    18, Acts 13:2, 14:23.*
5   *Paul said 'I beat my body and make it my slave' (1
    Corinthians 9:27). How does this verse apply to Christians
    in the 21st century? How will you personally apply it
    during this period of Lent?*

4. 'For Christ's Sake, Excellence'

by Os Guinness

Once, when Winston Churchill was on holiday staying with friends in the south of France, he came into the house on a chilly evening, sat down by the fireplace, and stared silently into the flames. Resin-filled pine logs were crackling, hissing, and spitting as they burned. Suddenly his familiar voice growled, 'I know why logs spit. I know what it is to be consumed.'

Human beings consume and are consumed by many things – food, drink, possessions, ambition, love, to name a few. Many of these things only shrink and debase us. But in the great person and with the great cause, the consuming force may become a magnificent obsession and a heroic destiny.

Winston Churchill himself was consumed by an extraordinary sense of providence and personal destiny – leading a nation and championing the cause of freedom against a vile tyranny at overwhelming odds. On the night of May 10, 1940, Churchill was invited by King George VI to form a government and lead Britain against the forces of Nazism that menaced Europe and threatened the free democracies. Churchill later recounted, 'I felt as if I were walking with destiny, and that all my past life had been but a preparation for this hour and for this trial.'

For some people the grand passion is art, music, or literature; for others the dream of freedom and justice; for yet others the love of a man or a woman. But search as you will, there is no higher or more ultimate passion than a human being ablaze with a desire for God.

Moses was such a person. By nature he was a man of action and not, as he said to God, 'a man of words.' He was transformed as he learned the failure of his own self-styled actions and the power of his halting words when they come from God himself. Twice he reverted to character as a man of action, once striking an Egyptian dead and once striking the rock to produce water. The first action turned out to be a failure; the second an act of disobedience.

Slowly, incident by incident, test by test, Moses was shaped to be a man of God and a prophet, a hero of the moral word. Supremely, facing the rebellion of the Golden Calf in the deepest crisis of his life, with his own survival as well as his leadership on the line, he prayed audaciously to know all of God that God will allow and a fallen human being can stand to know. 'Lord, show me your glory,' he asked and his request was granted. From then on his eyes had quite literally seen the glory of the coming of the Lord and he lived to tell the story.

Little wonder Moses was later given the tribute, 'Since then, no prophet has risen in Israel like Moses, whom the Lord knew face to face.' But how was this great intimate of God called? He was arrested at the sight of a bush, burning yet not burned up – as if God were telling him from the very beginning that his call would set his life on fire, but the fire would not consume him.

Nearer our own time Blaise Pascal was another such person on fire with passion for God. Mathematical genius, inventor, grandfather of the computer and modern risk theory, renaissance thinker well versed in physics, philosophy, and theology as well as mathematics, among the most elegant prose stylists in the French language, Pascal is one of the supreme human thinkers of all time and author of a great masterpiece of Western literature – *Pensées.*

But almost no one in Pascal's day and still too few in ours know of the experience that kept these achievements in perspective and lay at the core of his brief, intense, pain-filled, flame burst of a life. On the evening of Monday, November 23, 1654, he was thirty-one years old and had just experienced a close brush with death in a carriage driving accident. That night he had a profound encounter with God that changed the course of his life. Pascal was a notoriously fast driver and sceptics were ready with their scorn. 'My friend,' Voltaire scoffed to Condorcet, 'never weary saying that since the accident on the Neuilly Bridge, Pascal's brain was damaged!'

Pascal's experience lasted from 10:30 p.m. until 12:30 a.m. It is often called his 'second conversion,' to distinguish it from his first, more formal conversion at Rouen when he was twenty-four. What he went through strained and finally shattered the capacities of his language. He could only title it in one word: *fire.* But the experience was so precious and decisive to him that he sewed the parchment record of it into the lining of his doublet and wore it next to his heart. For the remaining eight years of his life he took the trouble to sew it into every new doublet he bought, and it was only found by his sister, who felt the odd bump it formed, after his death in 1662 at the age of thirty-nine. The opening half of his 'Memorial' reads:

Fire

> 'God of Abraham, God of Isaac, God of Jacob,'
>   not of philosophers and scholars.
> Certainty, certainty, heartfelt, joy, peace.
> God of Jesus Christ.
> God of Jesus Christ.
> My God and Your God.
> 'Your God shall be my God.'
> The world forgotten, and everything except God.
> He can only be found by the ways taught in the Gospels.
> Greatness of the human soul.
> 'O righteous father, the world had not known thee,
>   but I have known thee.'
> Joy, Joy, Joy, tears of joy.

Most of us cannot begin to understand Pascal's mathematical accomplishments, and we would not wish to experience the pain and suffering of his short life. But what lit and fanned into a blaze the deep potential of his character and gifts is something open to us all – the call of God. The call came to Pascal so deeply that he became a man consumed by a divine fire that touched his life and work. As such Pascal illustrates a further aspect of the wonder of calling – *God's calling is the key to igniting a passion for the deepest growth and highest heroism in life.*

Heroism, it is often said, has fallen on hard times in the modern world. Many reasons have been given, but two are especially prominent. One is the modern habit of debunking. Aleksandr Solzhenitsyn described Stalin as so suspicious that 'mistrust was his worldview.' But following the three grand masters of suspicion, Nietzsche, Marx, and Freud, we have all been schooled in the art of mistrust. Heroism is therefore automatically suspect today. As modern people, we look straightaway not for the golden aura but for the feet of clay, not for the stirring example but for the cynical motive, not for the ideal embodied but for the energetic press agent.

Only then, we say to ourselves, will we know we are not being duped. But the trouble is, only rarely do we suspend disbelief. So even if there are genuine heroes today, it is difficult for us to admire them long enough to emulate them.

The other reason commonly given for the crisis of heroism is that, in fact, there are fewer heroes – because of the role of the press and media in creating the modern celebrity and widening the gap between fame and greatness, heroism and accomplishment. Formerly, it is pointed out, heroism was linked to the honour of accomplishment. Honour was accorded to the person with some genuine achievement, whether in character, virtue, wisdom, the arts, sport, or warfare.

Today, however, the media offer a shortcut to fame – instantly fabricated famousness with no need for the sweat, cost, and dedication of true greatness. The result is not the hero but the celebrity, the person famously described as 'well-known for being well-known.' A big name rather than a big person, the celebrity is someone for whom character is nothing, coverage is all.

Powerful and important though they are, these two factors pale beside a third reason for the crisis of heroism – the so-called death of God in western society or what should be termed more accurately the drowning out of the call of God in modern life.

Psychologist Ernest Becker clearly recognized this problem. In his book *The Denial of Death* he acknowledged: 'One can only talk about an ideal human character from a perspective of absolute transcendence.' Becker therefore saw that Søren Kierkegaard's formula for what it means to be a man was apt and inspiring. To

be a great human being was to be 'a knight of faith,'
which Becker describes sympathetically:

> This figure is the man who lives in faith, who has given over
> the meaning of his life to his Creator, and who lives centered
> on the energies of his Creator. He accepts whatever happens
> in this visible dimension without complaint, lives his life as
> a duty, faces his death without a qualm. No pettiness is so
> petty that it threatens his meanings; no task is too
> frightening to be beyond his courage. He is fully in the
> world on its terms and wholly beyond the world in his trust
> in the invisible dimension.

Becker readily acknowledged the beauty of this calling.
The knight of faith is 'surely one of the most beautiful
and challenging ideals ever put forth by man.' But he
concluded sadly, 'One cannot give the gifts of the knight
of faith without first being dubbed by some Higher
Majesty.' Just as there is no calling without a Caller and
no age of faith unless the purpose of life is placed beyond
life, so – for people without God – there are no knights of
faith because there is no Higher Majesty to dub them.

But what of the person of faith whose life is an answer
to the call of God, who has been dubbed by a Higher
Majesty? Following the call becomes the secret of growth
and a key to heroism in two ways. First, God's call always
challenges us directly to rise to our full stature as human
beings. Human beings who come face to face with the
presence and call of God typically react like many in the
Old Testament – falling flat on their faces in awe and
wonder. But when they do, God's response is to say, as to
Ezekiel at his call, 'Stand up on your feet and I will speak
to you.'

In other words, there is more to God's call than simply
sending us out – the commissioning, as calling is usually

thought to be. Certainly, it ends by 'sending us out,' but it begins by 'singling us out' – we are called by name – and it continues by 'standing us up.' As we respond to the call of our Creator, we rise to our feet, not only physically but also in every sense of the word, to be the people he alone knows we are capable of being. Like a coach bringing out the full capacity of each member of the team, or a conductor bringing out the deepest potential of the orchestra, God's call resonates in us at depths no other call can reach and draws us on and out and up to heights no other call can scale or see.

C. S. Lewis well captures this thrilling theme. The higher and different sort of life of God's call is as far above normal life, as spiritual life is above biological life. Certainly there is a resemblance, as between a photo and a place, or a statue and a man. But someone rising to the call and passing from the biological life to the spiritual life 'would have gone through as big a change as a statue which changed from being a carved stone to being a real man. And that is precisely what Christianity is about. This world is a great sculptor's shop. We are the statues and there is a rumour going round the shop that some of us are some day going to come to life.'

Second, God's call to follow him is vital to growth and heroism because it includes the element of imitation that is at its heart. Even with human heroism, the hero is the person of worth on whom we model our lives and pour forth our surging aspirations, and thereby grow higher than we ever would on our own. But merely human heroes are always fallible, sometimes disappointing, and they often compete with our other heroes for our loyalty. Concerning them we can agree with Nietzsche: 'One repays a teacher badly if one always remains a pupil only.' Jesus Christ, fully God and fully man, is the one true hero. He alone will never be surpassed, but neither will we surpass what we grow to be if we model ourselves on him.

Following God's call therefore says that as we run the race of faith, 'let us fix our eyes on Jesus, the author and perfecter of our faith' – the Greek word for pattern and role model. Similarly, the apostle Paul wrote to the disciples in Corinth, 'Be imitators of me as I am of Christ.' Or as Dostoevsky's Father Zossima said, 'What is Christ's word without an example?'

Paul's use of the word *imitators* is important. Modelling – observing and copying – is vital to disciple- ship because of the biblical view of the way disciples must learn. There is always more to knowing than human knowing will ever know. So the deepest know- ledge can never be put into words – or spelled out in sermons, books, lectures, and seminars. It must be learned from the Master, under his authority, in experience. When we read in the Gospels that Jesus chose twelve 'to be with him,' their being with him was not some extra privilege they enjoyed. It was the heart and soul of their discipleship and learning.

The theme of tutoring and imitation, which goes far deeper than current notions of 'mentoring,' is conspicuous in the teaching of the early church. We grow through copying deeds not just listening to words, through example as well as precept, through habit and not just insight and information. Calling therefore creates an ethic of aspiration, not just of obligation. Ignatius of Antioch urged the Philadelphians 'to imitate Jesus Christ as he imitated the Father.' Clement of Alexandria wrote, 'Our tutor Jesus Christ exemplifies the true life and trains the one who is in Christ … He gives commands and embodies the commands that we might be able to accomplish them.'

Clement's last sentence is noteworthy. Some Christians are suspicious of imitation because it sounds like a form of self-help spirituality. Modelling seems to smack of a foolproof method of growth that is as mechanical as the instructions for assembling a model airplane. But they misunderstand imitation. For one thing, genuine 'originality' is God's prerogative, not ours. At our most 'creative,' we are only imitative. For another, imitating a life is far from wooden. Real lives touch us profoundly – they stir, challenge, rebuke, shame, amuse, and inspire at levels of which we are hardly aware. That is why biographies are the literature of calling; few things are less mechanical.

No one apart from Jesus and Paul has been more influential on the church than Augustine. Not only do we have his many writings but we also have his unique *Confessions*. Yet when Augustine died, his contemporaries, who also knew his live sermons, appreciated most of all his life. His friend Possidius wrote: 'Yet I think that those who gained most from him were those who had been able actually to see and hear him as he spoke in Church, and, most of all, those who had some contact with the quality of his life among men.'

Importantly, imitating Christ is not a form of do-it-yourself change because it is part and parcel of responding to the call – a decisive divine word whose creative power is the deepest secret of the change. Think of Ezekiel's vision of the valley of the dry bones or the astounding miracle of Jesus calling the dead Lazarus out of the tomb. Can anyone listen to that voice, see what it effects, and still say the hearers responded by themselves? Do dry, brittle bones ever reassemble into a body on their own? Can a corpse shake off death by itself?

No more do we change by ourselves as we imitate Christ. The imitation of Christ that is integral to following him means that, when he calls us, he enables us to do what he calls us to do.

Has anyone said it better than Oswald Chambers in his matchless description of the disciple's master passion, 'My utmost for his highest'? Often I hear it said that Christians have no equivalent of the Greek notion of excellence – the ideal that each person or thing is to achieve the highest standard of perfection of which it is capable. That is not true. However, the pursuit of excellence that for the Greeks could be achieved by human endeavour alone is only possible for the follower of Christ in response to the high call of God.

Do you long to rise to the full stature of whom you are created to be? To know the passion of the intensity of life at its fullest? To be your utmost for his highest? Listen to Jesus of Nazareth; answer his call.

Study Questions

1. *Look back over the chapter at the individuals Os Guinness refers to and the quotations he cites. Whose example inspired you most? Explain your answer.*
2. *In what specific ways has responding to God's call on your life and living in obedience to his will helped you grow spiritually? For example, explain how your spiritual gifts have developed, your faith grown stronger or your ambitions come into line with God's.*
3. *Choose a character from the Bible and reflect on their life in the light of Os Guinness' statement that 'God's calling is the key to igniting a passion for the deepest growth and highest heroism in life.'*

- Read the Bible passage which explains their calling
- How did obeying God's calling help them grow?
- How did a confidence in God's purposes help them act heroically in difficult circumstances?
- What were the main reasons for their failures?
- What lessons can we learn about how to define 'growth', 'heroism' and 'success'?

4. According to the writer what does imitating Christ involve and how does it bring about change in us?

5. Discuss together the particular difficulties you face in imitating Christ in your home and workplace. As a group share ideas and resources which could help address these issues and then individually determine what practical measures you are going to take during this Lent period.

5. The Secret of Wisdom

by Philip Baker

Wisdom is best defined not in theories, ideas or learning, but in the application of knowledge. Wisdom is action. The learned know, but the wise do. The power of one idea acted on today can affect millions tomorrow. There are many scholars and scientists whose theories are made impressive by book credits and degrees, but only a few are wise.

Dr Mohammed Yunus of the Grameen Bank in Bangladesh is one such individual. One day in 1976 this Economics Professor strolled through a small village in Bangladesh. He began speaking to a poor woman who was trying to make a living by selling bamboo stools. Although hard at work, she was only making two cents a day. Yunus discovered that the reason for her low profit margin was that she had no capital to buy her own bamboo, so the money was loaned to her by the trader who purchased the final product. The interest charged by the trader essentially removed her profit margin.

On further enquiry the same scenario was repeated in many families within the same village. When Yunus looked at the figures he was both shocked and motivated. Forty-two people were caught in this interest-driven bonded labour. Their freedom would come only if they could borrow the money from more traditional sources. The total amount in question to empower these forty-two people was 856 Takas, about $26.00.

Years later in testifying before the US Congress Select Committee on Hunger, Yunus recalled his intense emotions during this watershed experience: 'I felt extremely ashamed of myself, being part of a society which could not provide $26.00 to forty-two able, skilled human beings who were trying to make a living'.[1]

From this genesis the Grameen (which means village) Bank was founded. Its purpose was to loan money to poor people who had no collateral. The results have been staggering. Over the past two decades, the bank has extended loans in excess of 1.5 billion dollars to some of the poorest people in the world. The bank today serves some two million clients, 94 per cent of them women, with a repayment rate of 97 per cent. Wisdom, when put to work, works.

The wise man in Jesus' parable of the house built on the rock was wise simply because he heard truth and then did something about it. The foolish man is the one who 'hears the words of mine and does not put them into practice.'[2]

Notice that a person is not just wise because they do, but because they hear and do. Wisdom requires input, but it is input with intention. Learning with purpose. Studying for its own sake, like any hobby, may be relaxing and fulfilling but does not equal wisdom. It is simply stage one in a two-stage process.

In business, it is not those who have ideas who create profit or change, but those who act on their ideas. We

[1]Bornstein, D., *The Price of a Dream* (University Press Ltd., Dhaka,1996), p30.
[2]Matthew 7:26

have all had the experience of seeing one of 'our' ideas, which came to us in a quiet moment but remained simply a muse, acted on by another.

I remember my father being mildly upset when a restaurant started putting photographs in their menus. 'My idea. I could have made money if I had gone into this line of business.' My ideas have been similarly hijacked. I mean who of us didn't think of Pet Rocks, Hula Hoops, Trivial Pursuit or the concept of franchising?! Others have had these same thoughts but then decided to do something about them. Doing makes the difference.

Matsushita, probably the greatest entrepreneur of this century, started off by taking this risk of doing. He quit his secure job when just a young man, because his boss disagreed with his idea of creating a new type of light socket. He began to manufacture the product himself. The rest is writ large in the annals of business history. His company now employs 265,000 workers with revenues of 63 billion dollars. Wisdom is seen, not in Harvard or Stanford degrees, but in pragmatic application of well-researched and heartfelt conviction.

Knowledge alone is impotent to change a life. We learn and know, but if we do not act and make a habit of such inaction, we are doomed to discontentment and frustration. We know, but others succeed.

The mere gatherer of ideas will never see the power of wisdom unless they begin to sow in action. Freud smoked so many cigars that he finally had to have the roof of his mouth cut out, and still he could not stop. His biographer, Peter Gay, points out: 'Freud's inability to give up smoking vividly underscores the truth in his observation of an all-too-human disposition he called knowing and not knowing. A state of rational apprehension that does not result in appropriate behaviour'.[3]

[3]Gay, P., *Freud: A Life for Our Time* (Norton, New York).

F. W. Woolworth is another example of the power of creativity coupled with wise action. He was working as a clerk in a hardware store when his boss began to complain about the piles of out-of-date goods that were not selling. Woolworth's idea was to set up a separate table and price everything at ten cents. Very soon the table became the most profitable area of the store. Woolworth then had the confidence and the wisdom to apply his new idea to an entire store. His boss, however, did not. The Woolworth chain of five-and-dimes quickly spread across America earning him, in the process, a fortune. His former boss once commented: 'Every word I used in turning that man's offer down has cost me about a million dollars I might have earned.'[4]

This characteristic of wisdom has been amply delineated by many writers and speakers. Aristotle to Shakespeare, the Bible to Norman Vincent Peale. Yet we still find it difficult to comprehend. 'Surely there must be more to success than simply doing', we muse. History teaches us, however, that one can lack a high IQ, magnetic personality, or magnificent skill, but if we do something rather than just think about it, a mark is made for all to see.

Often the one most amazed is the doer themselves. William Barclay, a well-known theological writer, is clear evidence of this truth. He was originally approached by Saint Andrew Press, who were wanting to produce a series of Bible commentaries written for the layperson. They asked him whether he would carry out the assignment until they 'found someone good'. (Barclay was a relatively unknown cleric at the time.) It seemed they never could find anyone who was good, and Barclay continued writing until he had finished the entire New

[4]*Napoleon Hill's Keys to Success*, Editor – Matthew Sartwell (Piatkus, London, 1994), p168

Testament. He often made the point that the reason he had been successful was not because he was a wonderful writer or thinker. He admitted there were thousands of others in England alone who had more to say and were better at saying it. The only difference between him and them was that he sat and wrote and they did not. His wife was a useful ally on this point, as she wouldn't let him out of his study for lunch until he had finished so many lines.

The same can be said for American Bob Richards, the 1956 Olympic Gold Medal winner in the pole vault. I once heard him say, in an after-dinner speech, that he thought there were a million other men in America who could have beaten him in his event. If raw talent alone was enough he would never have made it to the state championship let alone the Olympics. The story of his life, and many like him, illustrates that success is about what we do with what we have. It is action, not just gifting, the practice and not merely the theory. It is in the arena of action where the wise of heart discover the fruits of wisdom. I am not saying that doing is the only thing. Yet the point of action cannot be overstressed.

There seems to be something about the concept of wisdom that automatically causes us to picture it only in the study or the library. Wisdom personified is usually the professor from *Back to the Future* or 'Brains' from *Thunderbirds*, the bald head of large proportions, the long straggly beard, and the smudges of four-day-old coffee on the jacket. We think these are all dead giveaways to wisdom dwelling within. In reality, however, wisdom comes in varied garb. It is the fourteen-year-old who is motivated by the plight of extinction-threatened tigers, who rallies support from parents, friends, companies and the media, and successfully begins a foundation that actively and practically begins to address the situation. It is the twenty-two-year old young lady from New Zealand who takes the plunge and, with everything she has, launches a computer company just after the stock market crash of 1987. Today her net worth is in the multiple millions simply because of her actions. It is the young American accountant who, because he was unhappy with the council service, won the contract to pick up the garbage in his small suburb. Step by step the small firm grew and was sold several decades later for three hundred and fifty million dollars. All of these real-life examples have come across my path in the last few days. Given time, and a few thousand pages, we could continue in such a vein!

The evidence seems extensive. The best idea in the world not acted upon, is merely the idle chatter of the mind. It fills the time but produces nothing. Like trees that fall in the forest when no one is present, so the brainwave without application crashes silently on the shore.

This is not to suggest that wisdom's actions are always productive. Ideas fail, and promising pathways lead to dead ends. The wise, however, are not put off by the small inconvenience of failure. They merely continue to do. Sooner or later the rewards will come. Like the seed in the parable of the sower, some actions die immediately, others start with promise but then shrink and cease when placed under the pressure of the real world, whilst still others have their life drained away slowly as competing forces work against them. But some begin to grow and bear fruit, maybe a little, maybe a lot. If we assume that the four types of soil in the parable all received an equal amount of seed, then we note that only twenty-five per cent of that which was sown produced the fruit, and of that twenty-five per cent, one-third produced the most fruit. 'Some thirty-fold, some sixty-fold, some one hundred-fold.'[5]

When one does the maths, this equates to fifty-three per cent of the harvest coming from just eight per cent of the seed. From the sower's point of view, though, he is never sure which eight per cent will do the job. The rewards may be mediocre, moderate or magnificent. Yet we must continue to sow the seeds of action in our life, for then a harvest of peace and prosperity will be almost inevitable.

The wise, however, unlike the farmer, cannot be judged simply on the harvest. It is the act of doing, not the results of doing, where wisdom is best revealed. Edison's wisdom is seen in the thousands of failed experiments, not just the one that worked. Abraham Lincoln's wisdom was heralded by his growing and impressive list of failures. As he himself once said, 'Success is the ability to go from one failure to the next without losing enthusiasm!' The wise are the ones who are on the road. Destinations reached simply speak of miles travelled.

The road winds on and on. The wise of heart do not falter or return, for the road is right and the journey is fun. The meaning and the thrill are in the process. Some, sadly, never live to see the destination that their words and work finally reached. If they had, it would have proved only a small reward, for wisdom itself provides its own nourishment.

Study Questions

1   *Which of the individuals Baker cites impressed you most? Explain your choice to the group.*

[5]Mark 4:20

2 Baker says 'The wise are not put off by the inconvenience of failure.' But often churches don't know how to react to moral failures and are scared to take risks in case of ministry failure. What guidelines would you suggest so that the church responds wisely to failure within its community?

3 Scan Matthew 26-28, recalling the events of the Passion. In what ways did Jesus' actions and the actions he instituted reveal his wisdom?

4 Lent is traditionally a time for reflection – but don't use that as an excuse for inaction! What one thing do you think God wants you to do for him? Consider your service for him in the home, workplace, church and community. How can you keep focused on your mission in the same way Jesus was?

5 Spend time personally confessing the specific occasions where 'we have left undone those things which we ought to have done; and we have done those things which we ought not to have done' (Book of Common Prayer).

6. Purposeful Living

by Philip Baker

Sometimes I lie awake at night and ask, 'Where have I gone wrong?' Then a voice says to me, 'This is going to take more than one night!'

Charlie Brown

The opening scene of *Forrest Gump* was lauded for its special effects wizardry. A computer-generated feather was superimposed on the scene in such a way that the audience believed the camera had caught its long, haphazard and spasmodic movement as it journeyed on the wind to finally come to rest on Forrest's shoe.

The feather, of course, was a metaphor. The winds of coincidence and the gusts of chance play a key role in who we are and what we do or don't do in life. However, unlike the feather, we can choose how we react to the 'slings and arrows of outrageous fortune'.[1]

We can use them to our advantage. In other words, we either use or are used.

The out-of-control life is the life that is responding rather than initiating. It is a life that simply happens rather than is caused. A life which gives in to the lie of fatalism and settles unquietly into the blame mentality.

[1]Shakespeare, *Hamlet*, Act 3, Scene 1

The truth about Forrest Gump was that he was in control. Other characters in the film with so much more to live for, were often not.

'*Que sera, sera, ...*' apologies to Doris Day, is no way to live. Whatever will be, will be, is to deny humanity the dignity of decision-making and intentional living. Surely destiny and vision have the power to transform lives. Surely choice changes circumstance. Yet we live in a society where many believe that their future is non-flexible, or if it is they are not the ones with the power to flex.

There is a truth that tells us to accept the facts and realise that there are some things we cannot change. This is wisdom indeed, and would keep us from the ditch of despair on the one hand and the dreamland of denial on the other. However, such wisdom may come with a sting in its tail. For who is to say what we can or cannot change? The black and whites are easy here, but most of life is in the grey. Accepting the death of a loved one or the process of aging (even though we fight to mitigate its effects) tend not to be confusing areas for the majority. Yet most of life is not as clear. Sadly, however, many place the majority of difficult and painful circumstances into this immutable category, thus avoiding responsibility and losing control.

Reinhold Niebuhr, a key Christian theologian in the 1940s and 1950s, once wrote on the back of an envelope a short prayer that sums up the dilemma we find ourselves in. It became the prayer of Alcoholics Anonymous and is familiar to us all:

> God, grant me the serenity to accept the things I cannot change, the courage to change the things I can, and the wisdom to know the difference.[2]

[2]As told in John Carmody, *How to Handle Trouble* (Doubleday, New York, 1993), p14

Granted, this type of discernment takes work and rigorous self-evaluation. It is a lot easier to sing with Mother Mary: 'Let it be, let it be.' Life, however, is to be lived. We are not meant to be just hitchhiking through our allotted span in these mortal vehicles. This is the passivist approach where life, rather than be caused, just happens. Floating downstream is enjoyable in the short term, but becomes soul-destroying in the long term. Significance and fulfilment are not found amongst those who spectate, but those who intentionally involve themselves in the process of existence.

This book is all about such purposeful living. Confronting these issues will quickly cause us to realise that the best view is from behind the driver's wheel and not from the back seat. My hope is that the reader will not only think about existence in new ways, but be empowered to practically act so that life is enriched and meaning and destiny are unearthed.

The desire to be in control of our own lives is healthy and sound. The desire to be in control of everyone else's life is not. Megalomaniacs and bossy demi-gods aside, the word 'control', when used in this personal sense is wholesome. Yet, this desire is relatively difficult to translate into reality. For many, the concept and dream of self-authority is a forlorn one. The pressures of conformity and the influence of poor self-esteem seem irresistible.

Some are even worse off. They suffer the illusion of self-control. They think they are in charge, but other forces are at work. Like the business person who works his or her way up the corporate ladder, unable to see the strings of materialism or prestige which jerk them ever upwards. Only later in life when the ladder top is reached, the discovery is made that it was leaning against the wrong wall.

These strings that bind us are often translucent and hard to spot. Yet we know they are there, for we do not do that which we desire.

Who do we blame

There seems to me a strange reluctance in our society today to own up to anything. Strange, in that ownership of the problem is also stage one in ownership of the answer. 'It's my fault. I take responsibility,' is not a statement that diminishes, it's a statement that empowers. On the other hand, the pointed finger, as Joseph Brodsky states, is the victim's logo.

The inability to 'fess up' is all too often a sign of personal complacency and an unwillingness to grow, yet grow we must if reaching our potential is our goal. The tragedy is that many do not realise how far they can go. They have settled for mediocrity and renamed it excellence. They compare only with those who are behind, never with those who are in front. Their hearts are like Japanese Bonsai trees. From close up they seem developed and fully grown, yet to those who look from a wider, more objective perspective, they see what really is, miniatures of what could and should be.

Such an attitude can only be maintained if we find someone or something else to take the rap. The following are the most frequent recipients of our misplaced accusations.

1. God

Homer, in the Odyssey, has Zeus complaining of how humanity point their fingers at the gods as the source of their troubles and suffering: 'It is through the blindness of the humans' hearts' or, as another translation puts it,

'Their greed and folly, that these things come upon them.'[3] Today is no different. Many choose the divine as an excuse for every type of failing or foolishness. Religion becomes the scapegoat upon which we send our volition and intelligence into the desert. Fatalism, and predestination, are allies in this process. These doctrines are, however, all too convenient. The wise heart recognises the truth that, if God is, then responsibility is both His gift and expectation. Free will is protected. We can choose to deny it and say it has been taken from us by the course of nature or by a capricious deity, but we are the ones who have to choose this escape ... Responsibility cannot so easily be given away.

2. Our Genes

Flip Wilson used to say, 'The Devil made me do it.' If this is true, then Satan has changed his name to 'gene', for genetics are more and more becoming the culprit for every form of human behaviour and misbehaviour. DNA has got a lot to answer for as it attempts to swing the nature versus nurture debate, putting its considerable weight behind the former.

Most prudent researchers and commentators on this issue would admit to both influences being powerful ones. Our genetics may mix the cement, but the resultant concrete remains wet for much of life. Our genes, it seems, can suggest things very strongly, but they lack the power to make the final act. I might put on weight more easily than you, but genetics don't make me fat, they only make my struggle with the second chocolate mousse more painful than yours, you skinny glutton! In the same

[3]Zeus, 'When It Is Through Blindness...', *Odyssey*, Book One, 30, as quoted by Barbara Tuchman, *The March of Folly* (Abacus, London, 1984), p55

way, the addictive personality cannot gain total escape from the prying cameras of responsibility by hiding. behind the screen of 'cellular make-up'. I may be weak, but I can still say 'no'. I may be ensnared, but help is normally as close as my choice. I may discover that my chemical make-up is such that one glass of wine is never enough, but I still can refuse that one glass.

In other words, genetic difference should cause us all to view one another with greater compassion. Wisdom does not crow over another's failing in an area of our strength, for we too have our foibles and need the understanding and help of others.

I hate to think what will happen if we begin to apply this new zeal for the chemical code to morality. Such a journey will prove to be on a slippery slope. The adulterer and murderer will breathe easier, but most of society will not. This approach would, however, explain a whole lot of problems. We might discover that our two-year-old is genetically disobedient, while the eighteen-year-old is genetically arrogant. I could point to my DNA as to why I forgot to take out the rubbish, or didn't hear my spouse during that important rugby game. Come to think of it, I'm in favour of this kind of argument. It means words like discipline, commitment, perseverance and courage can all be left on the side, for I sense my genes liberating me from such archaic concepts. Even the study of wisdom or foolishness is merely describing what is, and can never change what isn't.

The more one begins to think this way, the more the fallacy becomes obvious. A recent cartoon in *Newsweek* took this logic further. The picture showed a scientist rushing into a room full of his co-workers grouped around a microscope. 'Eureka!' he exclaimed.

'I've discovered the gene that makes us think that everything's determined by genes!'

Our nature does affect who we are. How could it do otherwise? Yet there is more to us than chemistry and, although genetics may speak to us via our feelings, to use them as our guide or our god is a tragic mistake of epic proportions. There may be nothing between Brooke Shields and her Calvin Kleins, but thank God there is a whole lot between us and our genes!

3. Circumstances

Much has been written on this particular substitute for responsibility. Zig Ziglar wrote at length, in his best-selling book *See You at the Top,* on the concept of loser's limps. That is, the tendency we all have to blame external circumstance for internal condition. These excuses to fail come in many and varied form: our upbringing, culture, colour, parentage, our lack or abundance of education, our height, size, beauty or ugliness. Anything can be used as an explanation to why we have not or will not achieve. Yet one of the most outstanding similarities that the majority of successful people share, as evidenced in various studies, is that they all have had major obstacles to overcome. In other words, environment or circumstance for them were more adverse than the average.

It seems that if the context of one's life is contrary, one can respond by either becoming a victim or by reaching deep into the heart and finding the necessary resources to overcome. Shakespeare had Hamlet make this point:

Whether tis nobler in the mind to suffer the slings and arrows of outrageous fortune or to take arms against a sea of troubles, and by opposing end them?[4]

Our environment is not us, the frame is not the picture, the table setting is not the food, and the screen is not the

[4]Shakespeare, Hamlet, Act 3, Scene 1

image. Life may have handed us nothing but pain, but, as Helen Keller found out, pain may prove to be a microphone that enables us to reach the world. In that knowledge we discover that our hurt diminishes as we play our part in diminishing it in the lives of others. Our hearts interpret our circumstances and can make a heaven out of hell or a hell out of heaven.

4. Fatalism

Fatalism carries one of the most depressing messages there is. If you're going to hang, you're not going to drown. No matter what you do or don't do, the results will remain the same. My attainment of wisdom or not is purely up to the giant hand in the sky, spirit of the cosmos, or the way of the world. Call it Gaia or Vishnu, Jehovah or 'the force', somebody out there somewhere is watching and controlling us. Free will is merely illusionary. Most people, however, don't buy into this completely. It is not uncommon to hear phrases like, 'It was meant to happen,' or, 'I guess things just weren't meant to be.' In other words, we adapt the philosophy of fatalism so that it affects the large things (marriage, success, premature death and the like) but choose not to apply it to the small things ('Can you pass the salt?', 'Let's go to the zoo today' and 'I think I will go to bed now.'). I have trouble with this. Either fatalism is true the whole way or not at all. If we are puppets, then why are we allowed to think for ourselves about anything?

In reality, those who hold to these views, more often than not, do not do so out of firm conviction, but out of convenience or superstition. When things don't work out I can easily blame fate, and so I am off the hook. Thus we avoid the responsibility of our actions and, so the theory goes, become free and happy. Yet, freedom from responsibility is not true freedom. The lion in the cage may be free from the worry of where the next meal will come from, or whether he will survive the drought. He is released from the burden of choice that is involved in planning his day. Yet such responsibilities are the stuff of freedom. Those who choose to escape these demands simply become the most bound of all.

In the same way as the lion is designed for the sweeping plains, and the bird to fly across the expanse of the wide horizon, so we have been designed to live and to choose. With this comes both the potential for right choice and the potential for wrong. We have the ability to sense pleasure, but also to feel pain. The truth is we cannot have one without the other. Probably Shackleton, after his expeditions in Antarctica, put this best:

> In memories we are rich. We had pierced the veneer of outside things. We had suffered, starved and triumphed, grovelled yet grasped at glory, grown bigger in the bigness of life. We had seen God in his splendours, heard the text that nature renders. We had reached the naked soul of man.

Love is not possible in a world where acceptance and compassion is automatic. Forgiveness means nothing if I don't have the choice not to forgive. I can only sense the wonder of joy because I have experienced the depths of tragedy. All too often we want the sweet without the sour, interaction without contradiction, faith without doubt, and victory without the fight. If that kind of world could have been possible, or is out there somewhere waiting for us to discover it, then I'm not sure that I would want to go. This life may be tough, but it is certainly better than all the alternatives I can think of.

5. Luck

I'm not sure whether the concept of being lucky or unlucky is a variant of fatalism, or if fatalism is a variant of luck. Either way, both are used to escape the consequence of actions, or to negate blame. I am not saying that there is no such thing as luck, any more than I have suggested there is no such thing as God, circumstances, genetics or fate. (Well, actually I am saying there is no such thing as fate!) The question is whether luck is the sole, major or minor dispenser of what we find life delivering to us.

Most would agree it plays a part in the game of life. 'The harder I practice the luckier I get,' is true, and not just of golf. Yet to gamble our future on luck or fate is to give away the gift of responsibility and therefore to exist disillusioned and disempowered.

So then, we are on our own. Left to face the music without the comfort or luxury of being able to point our fingers at other people or forces. This naked stage must become our home. We must be our own prompt and critic. Others will be there when the time is right, but they are not there to live our life or take the brunt of our bitterness. This is what growing up is all about.

Thus, the wisdom of responsibility is both self-admonishing and self-correcting, and without it we are merely victims in a world that is unfair and doesn't care.

Study Questions

1   *Look at the list of who and what we blame for the output of our lives. Which item resonates most with you? What other items would you add?*

2   *The author talks about the desire and need to be in control of our own lives. How can we square this with the biblical command to let God be in control of our lives? Is a balance possible?*

3   *The author explains that when we take responsibility and admit our failures we grow. In what ways have you seen this in your own spiritual life, even during the period of Lent?*

4   *In what issues do you think Christians need to take their gift of responsibility more seriously? Consider for example our social responsibility and our role as citizens of the world.*

5   *Reinhold Niebuhr wrote, 'God, grant me the serenity to accept the things I cannot change, the courage to change the things I can, and the wisdom to know the difference.' If it is appropriate, share in twos how this prayer specifically applies to your life. Spend time praying for each other.*

7. 'Who's Pulling Your Strings?'

by R.T. Kendall

Peter's sermon on the day of Pentecost was climaxed by 3,000 people being converted. Something we should all want to think about. Who was Peter? He was one of the twelve, he had left all to follow Jesus. He was without doubt the most colourful of the twelve – I would call him a man's man. He's the type of person you'd enjoy being with on a holiday, yet it must be said that he was a fallible man. When he was in the flesh, he was in the flesh. When he was in the Spirit, he was in the Spirit, and yet it seems nobody could get in the flesh like Peter could. You would have thought that if you were on the top of the mountain where Jesus was transfigured before Peter, James and John, that there would be such a sense of God's presence and therefore such presence of mind that no one could make a mistake; but Peter did. He said, 'Lord, it is good for us to be here. If you wish, I will put up three shelters – one for you, one for Moses and one for Elijah' (see Mt. 17:4). It was amazing that he could do that, but it shows that one can be in the flesh even in the presence of glory.

We know about that very sad moment when cowardly Peter denied even knowing the Lord. Using language he hadn't used in years and cursing before a servant girl, he claimed he didn't know Jesus. But when Peter was in the Spirit, he was in the Spirit. One day, Jesus said, 'Peter, who do you say that I am?' and Peter replied 'You are the Christ, the Son of the living God.' This was one time when Jesus could say, 'This was not revealed to you by man, but by my Father in heaven' (Mt. 16:17).

Peter was in the Spirit on the day of Pentecost. I think the key to what was going on here was the fact that he was a forgiven man. Only fifty days before, he had denied Christ, and now here he stands before thousands of people, we don't know how many, undoubtedly far more were present than the 3,000 that were converted, and preaches with such authority and with such power.

Peter was acutely conscious of having been forgiven. He had said to Jesus he would follow him all the way, and Jesus replied, 'Before the cock crows you will disown me', and Peter said, 'You don't know me Lord, I love you', and Jesus said 'Oh yes, you will'. When there was the crowing of the cockerel, Peter realised what he had done and he looked at Jesus, and Jesus was looking at him, and Peter went out and wept bitterly. On the day Jesus was raised from the dead he sent a special message to Peter, and now on the day of Pentecost, Peter has no reason for being self-righteous. He was aware of what he had done and I think that it is part of the key to his power: he knew he had no right to be there. One reason we ministers so often have no power is because we feel so self-righteous. I know what it is to have a week where I thought I was walking in the light and was free of any bitterness or grudge and I thought, 'This Sunday, I am going to have a great day.' I get in the pulpit feeling so good in myself – and I fall flat. And I know what it is to walk into the pulpit on a Sunday feeling so unworthy; maybe it was a busy week and I hadn't been able to pray much, or sometimes just before the service something will happen at home, perhaps my wife and I will be in an argument and I'll get upset with her and feel awful for things that I've said; and then I go into the pulpit and I think to myself, 'I've no right to be here, I can't preach today', only to find that something takes over when I know that I've been forgiven.

Peter did not have a trace of self-righteousness in him that day; he was a forgiven man. But Peter was also the filled man, filled with the Spirit and chosen by the Holy Spirit to stand up and preach. Now all of the 120 were equally filled with the Holy Spirit, but I suspect not all could have done what Peter did. It's a mistake to think that if everybody is going to be filled with the Spirit, everybody can do the same thing. We all have our gifts and our personalities and God always wants us to be ourselves. Peter was the one that was chosen, filled with the Spirit, and perhaps the most remarkable thing about the day of Pentecost, other than the fact of three thousand being converted, was this – for the first time Peter and the other followers of Jesus in the upper room that day got it all together, for the very first time everything clicked.

Crucifixion confusion

Now the truth is, until that day, they did not really know who Jesus was. They could say the right words and know something of him being divine as Peter confessed, but it wasn't that clear to any of them; for one thing, Peter couldn't understand why Jesus died on the cross. There is an old spiritual we sing in the south of the States, 'Were you there when they crucified my Lord?' The truth is, you could have been there and not seen a thing. For had you

72 Approaching the Passion

been there, you would not have known by what you saw that God was in Christ reconciling the world to himself. You wouldn't have felt a thing. It was an awful sight, a crucifixion, cruel, horrible, awesome, and you would not have known that atonement was taking place. Even after Jesus was raised from the dead the disciples didn't really know why he had died. It wasn't clear to them. Thrilled though they were, the resurrection had not made it clear why he died.

In fact, there were mysterious things taking place over the next forty days. Jesus would show up and talk to the twelve or to the eleven and then he would disappear. Then, when they weren't thinking about it, here would come Jesus again and then he would vanish. One senses that the disciples began wondering what was going on. They were glad that he had been raised from the dead but didn't know what was happening and they all had one question on their minds. It was only a matter of time until it was asked and in Acts 1:6 they said to Jesus: 'Lord, are you at this time going to restore the kingdom to Israel?' That is what was on their minds; that is what they thought the Messiah had come to do. They saw the Messiah as being the deliverer who would emancipate Israel from Rome. Even though Jesus had died on the cross and was raised from the dead, they still thought this was the reason Jesus had come, and they wanted to know when it was all going to happen. Jesus replied, 'It is not for you to know the times or the dates the Father has set by his own authority. But you will receive power when the Holy Spirit comes on you; and you will be my witnesses in Jerusalem, and in all Judea and Samaria and to the ends of the earth.' This language was quite different and did not cohere with their idea of what the Messiah was to be like.

The last thing Jesus said to them was 'Wait, do not leave Jerusalem.' We don't know for sure how many heard him say that. We know from a comment made by the apostle Paul that at one time there were five hundred present who saw Jesus raised from the dead, but I don't know how many heard Jesus tell them to wait. All we do know is that 120 were waiting when the Holy Spirit came. If only Jesus had told them that the Spirit was going to come on the tenth day, and that would be the day of Pentecost, or that after forty days he was to be caught up in the clouds and ascend to heaven, to take his place at the right hand of God. No, the last word was 'Wait, don't leave Jerusalem.' But they didn't know whether it would be one day, two days or a hundred.

Surprise and stigma

I suspect that, the first day all five hundred or however many there were went to that place, they began to pray, excited, thinking that in hours something was going to happen. I suspect after a few days the numbers went down and I wouldn't be surprised if, on the day of Pentecost, there were those who said, 'I'm going to give this day a miss because there are so many people in Jerusalem today for this feast. We haven't seen them since last year and I will send my apologies, I'll come back tomorrow.'

But the faithful 120 were still there. We are told that 'When the day of Pentecost came they were all together in one place. Suddenly a sound like the blowing of a violent wind came' (2:1). Sometimes God works predictively, sometimes God works traditionally, but no one was really prepared for this, for Jesus had never said listen for the wind; he had never said watch for tongues of fire on each other's heads; he only said, 'Wait.' It's a reminder that whenever the Lord says to us 'Wait', this is a specific instruction and it means he's up to something: and if we don't wait we will be sorry. I'd hate to be one of those who missed it. But those who went as usual suddenly heard the sound of wind. They'd heard wind before, but this wind was different, an amazing sound, getting closer and closer to Jerusalem, and I imagine they began to ask 'Could this be it?' It was coming in the very direction of the upper room, that room that was so filled with memories. They began to notice something unusual.

Fifty days before these men and women had been demoralised. When they saw Jesus Christ on the cross it made no sense. They thought he was the one that would deliver Israel. They had seen him perform miracles, Peter saw him walk on water and Peter walked on water with him, they saw him raise Lazarus from the dead, they saw him feed the five thousand with the loaves and the fish; now there he was on the cross, it couldn't be happening. But suddenly everything is changed. 'Suddenly a sound like the blowing of a violent wind came and filled the whole house where they were sitting. They saw what seemed to be tongues of fire that separated and came to rest on each of them. All of them were filled with the Holy Spirit and began to speak in other tongues as the Spirit enabled them' (2:2-4). As they looked at each other they were filled with joy, no greater than which can be conceived and all they could think was, it's happening, this is real, it is happening and it was worth waiting for.

But what was happening also, that they couldn't have realised at the time, was that the Holy Spirit was ensuring that the church would not only be born in revival, but also be born with a stigma. A stigma is a mark, a public disgrace, something none of us wants. We'll do anything to avoid a stigma, any sense of embarrassment or offence. Many of us hope that the Spirit of God will come down upon our country and that there might be a great awakening, and we may hope that there will be such power that there will be no stigma, no offence. We hope there will be sudden vindication and all will see that there is a God in the heavens. But God wants a stigma to accompany his church. So that which was so marvellous was not received by the multitudes in the way that it was received by those filled with the Spirit. The people were all amazed (2:12), and they said '"What does this mean?" Some, however, made fun of them and said, "They have had too much wine."'

What a pity that this would be the first reaction to the church born in revival, that they would be regarded as drunk. But it's just a fact God always deposits a stigma with any great work that he does. The angel came to Joseph and said, 'Do not be afraid to take Mary home as your wife, because what is conceived in her is from the Holy Spirit. She will give birth to a son, and you are to give him the name Jesus, because he will save his people from their sins.' Yet Joseph and Mary were regarded in Nazareth as having a baby out of wedlock. Everyone knew that they weren't married and that she was with child and had the baby – a stigma. When Jesus chose the twelve disciples, he chose men that didn't do anything for the reputation of Jesus himself – a stigma. You know the church works overtime to erase the stigma, the very thing God wants. Look at the cross, what was more shameful than that? Jesus had promised to his followers of three years that if they followed him they would receive a hundredfold in this life and life everlasting to come. They had trusted those words and now here was

Jesus on a cross. Someone shouted up to him, 'Come down from the cross, if you are the Son of God' (Mt. 27:40). Some thought he might do just that. I expect there were some in the crowd who were nudging each other saying, 'Watch, he will come down from the cross, he's not going to die. This is the man who raised Lazarus from the dead, he's playing games with them, he's going to come down from the cross, you watch.' But he didn't. In fact he cried out 'My God, my God, why have you forsaken me?' (Mt. 27:46). People began to look at each other saying, 'Something's going wrong here.' Then he cried out, 'It is finished,' bowed his head, and gave up the ghost. The shame of it all: it didn't make sense. And the cross has always been a stigma.

Paul determined when he went to Corinth to know nothing among them save Jesus Christ and him crucified. We may think that we can go forward devoid of stigma, but God is concerned that we keep it, to keep us humble, and to remind us that we are not going to get our joy and satisfaction from people's applause. Jesus said, 'How can you believe if you accept praise from one another, yet make no effort to obtain the praise that comes from the only God?' (Jn. 5:44).

The immediate reaction to the filling of the Spirit was predictable confusion. It almost always is, and as we look at the sermon of Peter and what takes place in these verses from Acts 2:14-41, we can summarise it in three stages – firstly, Peter's explanation; secondly, his exposition; and then thirdly, the effect of the sermon.

Peter's explanation

Here was Peter, fallible man, forgiven man, filled man; filled with the Spirit which enabled him for the first time to understand it all. It wasn't until then that it all fell into

place – why Jesus died, why he was raised from the dead.
Full of the, Spirit, the penny dropped, presence of mind
came, it all made sense. Jesus was God as though he were
not man, he was man as though he were not God. And
when he was dying on the cross, it was God punishing
Jesus for our sins. He took our place, and at long last
everything that Jesus had been saying – the parables, the
teachings – came together. Peter had authority, but we
must say he was filled with the Scriptures, for, having
been called upon to give an explanation, he said, 'Fellow
Jews and all of you who live in Jerusalem, let me explain
this to you; listen carefully to what I say. These men are
not drunk, as you suppose. It's only nine in the morning!
No, this is what was spoken by the prophet Joel: "In the
last days, God says, I will pour out my Spirit on all
people. Your sons and daughters will prophesy, your
young men will see visions and your old men will dream
dreams"' Full of the Scriptures, so in the course of this
sermon Peter quoted from the prophecy of Joel, Psalm 16
and Psalm 110.

Why do you suppose Peter was able to do that? Clearly
he knew the Scriptures before that day. Jesus said in John
14 verse 26, 'The Counsellor, the Holy Spirit, whom the
Father will send in my name, will teach you all things
and will remind you of everything that I have said to
you.' When we are filled with the Spirit, the Spirit brings
to our remembrance what is already there. Never think
that if you get full of the Holy Spirit, you can suddenly
quote Scripture, you won't be able to do it unless you
knew the Scripture first. We all like to think that if we just
pray a little more or get filled with the Spirit, God is going
to put knowledge into our heads, but this isn't the way it
is. The Spirit enables us to remember what is there. There
are times when you may feel the drudgery of reading

your Bible or going to Bible study or having to memorise Scripture. But when you are filled with the Spirit, it is then that you will call to remembrance what you need.

But that is not all. By being filled with the Spirit the Scriptures now made sense. For Jesus had said in John 16:13, 'But when he, the Spirit of truth, comes, he will guide you into all truth.' The only way we can understand the Scriptures is that the Holy Spirit is our guide, and humbling though it may be for us to have to admit, we all need to be guided. We may think it will be our great brain that will cause the Scriptures to unfold by themselves, but that's not the way it is. Let me tell you my favourite story which illustrates this point.

Many years ago I began to hear of bonefishing. There was something about catching a bonefish which had a ring to it because I had been told it was quite an accomplishment. No one should go without a guide, because the fish are very hard to catch and very difficult to see. The idea is that you don't just throw out your line and wait for the fish to pick up the bait, but you look for the fish. It's the only sport that simultaneously combines hunting and fishing. You literally look for the fish in crystal clear water. It's very shallow water, maybe twelve inches deep, and you look for a fish in the water, but they're very skittish and the slightest sound causes them to take off like a torpedo, so you've got to be very quiet. I was fascinated by that so I said I was going to go bonefishing, and my friend who was with me told me I shouldn't go without a guide. I said, 'Well, I've read a couple of articles in fishing magazines. I think I know what to do.'

'I think you're wrong', he said. 'You need a guide.'

I went to the fishing camp and I said to the manager, 'I want to go bonefishing.'

He said, 'Who's your guide?'

I said 'I don't have a guide.'

He said, 'Are you a bonefisherman?'

I said, 'Will be after today.'

He said, 'Have you ever been bonefishing before?'

I said,'No.'

He said, 'Nobody goes bonefishing without a guide.'

'Look,' I said, 'I'll be all right, will you rent me a boat?'

'Sure I'll rent you a boat,' he said

I said, 'Will you just tell me where to go?'

So he got a map, he told me where I would find thousands of bonefish.

I took the boat out all by myself and I began to look. I started out at 8 o'clock in the morning, I came back at 8 o'clock at night, and went to the manager of the fishing camp.

He said 'How many did you catch?'

I said, 'There weren't any.'

He said he thought there were and told me to go and have a look in the ice house. I went and there was a big bonefish that was prepared to be mounted.

I said, 'Where was it caught?'

He said, 'Right where you were, they were all around you.'

I said, 'I didn't even see any.'

'I told you you ought to have a guide,' he said.

That made me so mad I thought I'd never go bonefishing again. But a week or two later I thought I'd give it one more try, read one more article about what I was doing wrong. Do you know, the same thing happened. I didn't even see them. I'm ashamed to say how many weeks and months I went because I didn't want to pay the price of the guide and I didn't want to admit I had to have a guide. I've always been able to do things myself, thank you. But one day I finally knew I was beaten. We hired the best guide in the Florida Keys.

I said, 'Where shall we meet?'

He named the place – same as before.

I said, 'There's no use going there, I've been there for six months, there are no fish there.'

He said, 'Just be there.'

I was there. He started up the motor, chugged to the spot where I had been fishing for months, and turned off the motor.

He said, 'Shush, 10 o'clock, sixty feet to the stern of the boat.'

I said, 'Where? I don't see.'

'There he goes, nine pounder, see him?'

'No,' I said.

'It's all right, you'll see another one in a minute,' he said.

Five minutes later...

'Bonefish, 3 o'clock, coming across at 2, 1,' he said.

I still don't see it.

He said, 'All right, Kendall, there's a bonefish coming he's a hundred yards away, he's now at 12 o'clock, you just look at that spot at 2 o'clock.' He said '1, 1.30, there!' And I saw a dark shadow go across the spot.

So that's a bonefish! Before the day was over I actually hooked five for myself. What made the difference? I had to have a guide.

Paul says, 'The man without the Spirit does not accept the things that come from the Spirit of God, for they are foolishness to him' (1 Cor. 2:14), and we may think that because we've read one or two books we are going to understand the Bible. Maybe you are good in architecture, maybe you are good in history or philosophy, and then when it comes to the Bible, you read it and you say it makes no sense. But when the Spirit is come, you'll go back to the very same Scriptures which were a mystery to you and suddenly the meaning is unfolded. This is how it was that Peter, who hadn't understood anything until that day, was able to say that what the Bible said would happen was happening now.

Peter's exposition

The church was not only born in revival and born with a stigma, but it was born with expository preaching, and that is what Peter was doing on that day. At the end of the quotation of Joel came this, 'Everyone who calls on the name of the Lord shall be saved.' That was the key that led Peter to move in to what Jesus had come to do, to seek and to save that which was lost.

For Peter – forgiven man, filled man, full of the Spirit, full of the Scriptures – was also full of Jesus. There is the reason for his authority: he was full of Jesus. For now Jesus was as real to him in the Spirit as he had been to Peter in the flesh for the previous three years. When Jesus was saying that the Spirit would come he put it like this, 'In a little while you will see me no more, and then after a little while you will see me, because I am going to my Father.' The disciples got into a huddle and they said 'Did you hear that? A little while and we won't see him and a little while and we will. What does he mean?' These disciples were so depressed over everything that Jesus was saying about the Holy Spirit. In fact, Jesus said, 'Because I have said these things, you are filled with grief' (see Jn. 16). You couldn't have convinced them then that the Spirit would make Jesus so real to them that they would not even want to bring him back from heaven. But that's the way it was, and so full of Jesus was Peter that it was reflected on his face, so when he quoted Psalm 16 where David said, 'I saw the Lord always before me', Peter understood what that meant. For the whole time

Peter was preaching he was looking at Jesus, Jesus was right at his side, and the Lord was so real that Peter had an authority and a fearlessness. Jesus was more real to him than Peter's own existence. So Peter's message could be summarised by saying two things.

Peter's effect

First, something happened to Jesus and secondly, something happened to Peter. Verse 32, 'God has raised this Jesus to life, and we are all witnesses of the fact.' Something happened to Jesus, something happened to the disciples, and I suspect the audience was more interested in what had happened to them, because they were amazed that Peter could talk like this. They were amazed that this man, a fisherman, unlettered, regarded as ignorant by the priests, could speak with such boldness and honesty and with such a shine on his face. At that stage, they weren't all that interested in what had happened to Jesus, they didn't care anything about him. They didn't like him: they hated him, they didn't want his name mentioned. But they were interested in what had happened to Peter. That gripped them. We may think that the world is going to be interested in our Jesus, and we want them to be, but they're not going to be asking questions about him until they see that we are transformed, and that's what fascinated these people now. They were looking at Peter.

I never will forget how Arthur Blessitt had been walking through Amman, Jordan. Tired and thirsty, he put his cross down in front of the Holiday Inn in Amman. The place was being heavily guarded, and he found out later the OPEC ministers' conference was there. Arthur was surprised he got in, he was dirty, wearing jeans and a

T-shirt. He was thirsty so he went downstairs to the bar and asked for a coke, and was sitting at the end of the bar drinking his coke when an Arab sheikh walked over to him and said, 'I want what you've got'. Arthur asked him exactly what it was he meant. The Arab said that Arthur had something he wanted, there was a shine on Arthur's face. Arthur told him he was a follower of Jesus Christ and began to witness to him. The Arab prayed to receive Christ and it turned out he was an official with the OPEC ministers. For the next three days Arthur spent the whole time ministering to those oil men. They wouldn't have been interested in Jesus until they saw Arthur's face.

The multitude wanted to know how they could have what had happened to Peter. It was at this point Peter said, '"Repent. Change your mind. You need to change your mind about Jesus of Nazareth, because you took him and crucified him, but God has made that same Jesus, whom you crucified, both Lord and Christ. God allowed Jesus to be pierced and spat upon and hated, but now he has raised him from the dead, now Jesus is at the right hand of God, and God tells us to bow down to him. Repent, be baptised and you will receive the gift of the Holy Spirit." When the people heard this, they were cut to the heart.'

The Bible says that the word of God is quick, powerful, sharper than any two-edged sword, piercing even to the dividing asunder of soul and spirit and of the joints and marrow, and is a discerner of the thoughts and intents of the heart. Jesus said, 'When he, the Spirit of truth, comes, he will ... convict the world of guilt in regard to sin and righteousness and judgement.' It's the Spirit that makes a man see that he is lost. It's the Spirit that shows him his sin. It's the Spirit that convicts him of righteousness. It's the Spirit that lets him see there is judgement to come. The Spirit alone will convince people. We can argue until we're blue in the face – 'a man convinced against his will is of the same opinion still' – but when the Spirit is there, he will be cut to the heart and will say, 'What shall I do?' Nobody was laughing now. Nobody was mocking. They were convicted, concerned ('What shall we do?') and converted – it says they gladly received his word. Then they confessed, and as many as gladly received his word were baptised, right on the spot. Whoever came up with this idea that you wait months and years to be baptised after you've been converted? They did it right on the same day.

Who's pulling your strings? The Holy Spirit pulled the strings of Peter's heart; he obeyed the impulse of the Spirit and preached with power. The Spirit began to pull on the strings of the hearts of those who listened, and they realised that this was a very serious matter: What shall we do? Maybe you've seen Christianity as an optional thing and you have mocked and you've laughed. May God grant that the Spirit comes on you to convict and to give you a concern that you cry out 'What must I do?' because there is, most surely, judgement to come.

Study Questions

1 *Review the various functions of the Holy Spirit which Kendall mentions in this chapter. Which ones are most evident in your life, which ones would you like to see more of?*

2 *The author refers to Peter's lack of self-righteousness. Examining and removing self-righteousness is a key theme of Lent. What situations, thought-processes or activities encourage us to feel self-righteous? How can we counter these? Are there any verses in the Bible which offer guidance or help?*

3 Kendall writes 'The church works overtime to erase the stigma.' What stigmas should mark the Christian church in our generation and what is the evidence we're trying to erase them?

4 Why do you think Peter appreciated his forgiveness so much? Why do we often take our forgiveness for granted and consider it lightly? How can we correct our perspective?

5 How has this reminder of Pentecost helped you prepare for Easter? In what ways has it been valuable to look at the broader scope of God's salvation plan?

8. Keeping a Quiet Heart

by Elisabeth Elliott

Does God allow His children to be poor?

God allows both Christians and non-Christians to experience every form of suffering known to the human race, just as He allows His blessings to fall on both. Poverty, like other forms of suffering, is relative, as Lars and I were reminded while we were in India. Our country's definition of the 'poverty level' would mean unimaginable affluence to the girls we saw working next to our hotel. For nine hours a day they carried wet concrete in wooden basins on their heads, pouring it into the forms for the foundation of a large building. They were paid thirty cents a day.

On my list of Scriptures which give clues to some of God's reasons for allowing His children to suffer is 2 Corinthians 8:2: 'Somehow, in most difficult circumstances, their joy and the fact of being down to their last penny themselves, produced a magnificent concern for other people' (PHILLIPS). It was the Macedonian churches that Paul was talking about, living proof that it is not poverty or riches that determine generosity, and sometimes those who suffer the most financially are the ones most ready to share what they have. 'They simply begged us to accept their gifts and so let them share the honours of supporting their brothers in Christ' (v 4).

Money holds terrible power when it is loved. It can blind us, shackle us, fill us with anxiety and fear, torment our days and nights with misery, wear us out with chasing it. The Macedonian Christians, possessing little of it, accepted their lot with faith and trust. Their eyes were opened to see past their own misery. They saw what mattered far more than a bank account, and, out of 'magnificent concern,' contributed to the needs of their brothers.

If through losing what this world prizes we are enabled to gain what it despises – treasure in heaven, invisible and incorruptible – isn't it worth any kind of suffering? What is it worth to us to learn a little bit more of what the cross means – life out of death, the transformation of earth's losses and heartbreaks and tragedies?

Poverty has not been my experience, but God has allowed in the lives of each of us some sort of loss, the withdrawal of something we valued, in order that we may learn to offer ourselves a little more willingly, to allow the touch of death on one more thing we have clutched so tightly, and thus know fullness and freedom and joy that much sooner. We're not naturally inclined to love God and seek His Kingdom. Trouble may help to incline us – that is, it may tip us over, put some pressure on us, lean us in the right direction.

Why is God doing this to me?

An article appeared in the *National Geographic* years ago which has affected my thinking ever since. 'The

Incredible Universe,' by Kenneth F. Weaver and James P. Blair, included this paragraph:

> How can the human mind deal with the knowledge that the farthest object we can see in the universe is perhaps ten billion light years away! Imagine that the thickness of this page represents the distance from the earth to the sun (93,000,000 miles, or about eight light minutes). Then the distance to the nearest star ($4\frac{1}{3}$ light years) is a 71-foot-high stack of paper. And the diameter of our own galaxy (100,000 light years) is a 310-mile stack, while the edge of the known universe is not reached until the pile of paper is 31,000,000 miles high, a third of the way to the sun.

Thirty-one million miles. That's a very big stack of paper. By the time I get to thirty-one-and-a-half million I'm lost – aren't you? I read somewhere else that our galaxy is one (only one) of perhaps ten billion.

I know the One who made all that. He is my Shepherd. This is what He says: 'With my own hands I founded the earth, with my right hand I formed the expanse of sky; when I summoned them, they sprang at once into being ... I teach you for your own advantage and lead you in the way you must go. If only you had listened to my commands, your prosperity would have rolled on like a river in flood ...' (Isaiah 48:13, 17, 18, NEB).

Hardly a day goes by without my receiving a letter, a phone call, or a visit from someone in trouble. Almost always the question comes, in one form or another, *Why does God do this to me?*

When I am tempted to ask that same question, it loses its power when I remember that this Lord, into whose strong hands I long ago committed my life, is engineering a universe of unimaginable proportions and complexity.

How could I possibly understand all that He must take into consideration as He deals with it and with me, a single individual! He has given us countless assurances that we cannot get lost in the shuffle. He choreographs the 'molecular dance' which goes on every second of every minute of every day in every cell in the universe. For the record, *one* cell has about 200 trillion molecules. He makes note of the smallest seed and the tiniest sparrow. He is not too busy to keep records even of my falling hair.

Yet in our darkness we suppose He has overlooked us. He hasn't. I have been compiling a list of the answers God Himself has given us to our persistent question about adversity:

1. We need to be pruned. In Jesus' last discourse with His disciples before He was crucified (a discourse meant for us as well as for them), He explained that God is the gardener, He Himself is the vine, and we are branches. If we are bearing fruit, then we must be pruned. This is a painful process. Jesus knew that His disciples would face much suffering. He showed them, in this beautiful metaphor, that it was not for nothing. Only the well-pruned vine bears the best fruit. They could take comfort in knowing that the pruning proved they were neither barren nor withered, for in that case they would simply be burned up in the brushpile.

Pruning requires the cutting away not only of what is superfluous but also of what appears to be good stock. Why should we be so baffled when the Lord cuts away good things from our lives? He has explained why. 'This is my Father's glory, that you may bear fruit in plenty and so be my disciples' (John 15:8, NEB). We need not see *how* it works. He has told us it *does* work.

2. We need to be refined. Peter wrote to God's scattered people, reminding them that even though they were 'smarting for a little while under trials of many kinds' (they were in exile – the sort of trial most of us would think rather more than a 'smart'), they were nevertheless *chosen* in the purpose of God, *hallowed* to His service, and *consecrated* with the blood of Jesus Christ. With all that, they still needed refining. Gold is gold, but it has to go through fire. Faith is even more precious, so faith will always have another test to stand. Remember God's loving promise of 2 Corinthians 12:9, 'My grace is all you need; power comes to its full strength in weakness' (NEB).

> But Thou art making me, I thank Thee, sire.
> What Thou hast done and doest Thou knows't well.
> And I will help Thee; gently in Thy fire
> I will lie burning; on Thy potter's wheel
> I will whirl patient, though my brain should reel.
> Thy grace shall be enough the grief to quell,
> And growing strength perfect through weakness dire.

George MacDonald
Diary of an *Old Soul*, October 2

Ever been bitter?

Sometimes I've said, 'O Lord, you wouldn't do this to me, would you? How could you, Lord?' I can recall such times later on and realise that my perspective was skewed. One Scripture passage which helps me rectify it is Isaiah 45:9-11 (NEB): 'Will the pot contend with the potter, or the earthenware with the hand that shapes it? Will the clay ask the potter what he is making? ...Thus says the Lord, would you dare question me concerning my children, or instruct me in my handiwork? I alone, I made the earth and created man upon it.' He knows exactly what He is doing. I am *clay*. The word humble comes from the root word *humus*, earth, clay. Let me remember that when I question God's dealings. I don't understand Him, but then I'm not asked to understand, only to trust. Bitterness dissolves when I remember the kind of love with which He has loved me – He gave Himself for me. He gave Himself for me. *He gave Himself for me.* Whatever He is doing now, therefore, is not cause for bitterness. It has to be designed for good, because He loved me and gave Himself for me.

Is it a sin to ask God why?

It is always best to go first for our answers to Jesus Himself. He cried out on the cross, 'My God, my God, why have You forsaken me?' It was a human cry, a cry of desperation, springing from His heart's agony at the prospect of being put into the hands of wicked men and actually *becoming sin* for you and me. We can never suffer anything like that, yet we do at times feel forsaken and cry, *Why, Lord?*

The psalmist asked why. Job, a blameless man, suffering horrible torments on an ash heap, asked why. It does not seem to me to be sinful to ask the question. What is sinful is resentment against God and His dealings with us. When we begin to doubt His love and imagine that He is cheating us of something we have a right to, we are guilty as Adam and Eve were guilty. They took the snake at his word rather than God. The same snake comes to us repeatedly with the same suggestions: Does God love you? Does He really want the best for you? Is His word trustworthy? Isn't He cheating you? Forget His promises. You'd be better off if you do it your way.

I have often asked why. Many things have happened which I didn't plan on and which human rationality could not explain. In the darkness of my perplexity and sorrow I have heard Him say quietly, *Trust Me.* He knew that my question was not the challenge of unbelief or resentment. I have never doubted that He loves me, but I have sometimes felt like St. Teresa of Avila who, when she was dumped out of a carriage into a ditch, said, 'If this is the way You treat your friends, no wonder You have so few!' Job was not, it seems to me, a very patient man. But he never gave up his conviction that he was in God's hands. God was big enough to take whatever Job dished out (see Job 16 for a sample). Do not be afraid to tell Him exactly how you feel (He's already read your thoughts anyway). Don't tell the whole world. God can take it — others can't. Then listen for His answer. Six scriptural answers to the question WHY come from: 1 Peter 4:12-13; Romans 5:3-4; 2 Corinthians 12:9; John 14:31; Romans 8:17; Colossians 1:24. There is mystery, but it is not all mystery. Here are clear reasons.

Don't forfeit your peace

It would be impossible to exaggerate the importance hymns and spiritual songs have played in my spiritual growth. One of the latter, familiar to most of you, has this line: 'O what peace we often forfeit, O what needless pain we bear, all because we do not carry everything to God in prayer' (Joseph Scriven). Prayerlessness is one of the many ways we can forfeit the peace God wants us to have. I've been thinking of some other ways. Here's a sampling:

1. Resent God's ways.
2. Worry as much as possible.
3. Pray only about the things you can manage by yourself.

4. Refuse to accept what God gives.
5. Look for peace elsewhere than in Him.
6. Try to rule you own life.
7. Doubt God's word.
8. Carry all your cares.

If you'd rather *not* forfeit your peace, here are eight ways to find it (antidotes to the above eight):

1. 'Great peace have they which love thy law: and nothing shall offend them' (Psalm 119:165 KJV). 'Circumstances are the expression of God's will,' wrote Bishop Handley Moule.
2. 'Don't worry about anything whatever' (Philippians 4:6, PHILLIPS).
3. 'In everything make your requests known to God in prayer and petition with thanksgiving. Then the peace of God... will guard your hearts' (Philippians 4:6,7, NEB).
4. 'Take my yoke upon you and learn from me... and you will find rest' (Matthew 11:29, NIV).
5. 'Peace is my parting gift to you, my own peace, such as the world cannot give' (John 14:27, NEB).
6. 'Let the peace of Christ rule in your hearts' (Colossians 3:15, NIV).
7. 'May the God of hope fill you with all joy and peace in believing' (Romans 15:13, KJV).
8. 'Cast all your cares on him for you are his charge' (1 Peter 5:7, NEB).

Grant, O Lord my God, that I may never fall away in success or in failure; that I may not be prideful in prosperity nor dejected in adversity. Let me rejoice only in what unites us and sorrow only in what separates us. May I strive to please no one or fear to displease anyone except Yourself. May I seek always the things that are eternal and never those that are only temporal. May I shun any joy that is without You and never seek any that is beside You. O Lord, may I delight in any work I do for You and tire of any rest that is apart from You. My God, let me direct my heart towards You, and in my failings, always repent with a purpose of amendment.

St Thomas Aquinas

Study Questions

For each of the excerpts discuss what new perspective or fresh insight you gained from Elisabeth Elliot and then focus on the question specifically related to that section.

Does God allow his children to be poor?

1   *Speaking of the Macedonian Christians Paul said, 'Somehow, in most difficult circumstances, their joy and the fact of being down to their last penny themselves, produced a magnificent concern for other people' (2 Corinthians 8:2). What stops Christians today being generous financial givers? What needs to change for us to be more open-handed?*

Why is God doing this to me?

2   *Jesus also asked 'Why does God do this to me?' When he was on the cross he cried 'My God, My God, why have you forsaken me?' (Matthew 27:46). What do you imagine God's answer to Jesus would have been? How does God's answer and Jesus' own example help you cope with your own suffering?*

Ever been Bitter?

3   *Look up the scriptural principles the author gives for why God allows suffering and loss. What encouragement or challenge do these verses offer?*

Don't forfeit your peace

4 *Look at the author's first list – which of the ways do you most often forfeit God's peace? Discuss together practical suggestions of how you can appropriate the antidote, how can you make these Bible verses a reality in your life?*

9. The Oath of the Testimony

by Frank Morison

In attempting to unravel the tangled skein of passions, prejudices, and political intrigues with which the last days of Jesus are interwoven, it has always seemed to me a sound principle to go straight to the heart of the mystery by studying closely the nature of the charge which was brought against Him.

I remember this aspect of the question coming home to me one morning with new and unexpected force. I tried to picture to myself what would happen if some two thousand years hence a great controversy should arise about one who was the centre of a criminal trial, say, in 1922. By that time most of the essential documents would have passed into oblivion. An old faded cutting of *The Times* or *Telegraph*, or perhaps some tattered fragment of a legal book describing the case, might have survived to reach the collection of an antiquary. From these and other fragments the necessary conclusions would have to be drawn. Is it not certain that people living in that far-off day, and desiring to get at the real truth about the man concerned, would go first to the crucial question of the charge on which he was arraigned? They would say: 'What was all the trouble about? What did his accusers say and bring against him?' If, as in the present instance, several charges appear to have been preferred, they would ask what was the *real case* against the prisoner?

Directly we set this question in the forefront of our inquiry, certain things emerge which throw new and un-expected light upon the problem. It will help us to an understanding of what these significant things are if we consider first the very singular character of the trial itself. For not only did it take place at an unprecedented hour for such proceedings, but it was marked throughout by peculiarities of a special kind. Consider in the first instance the vital element of time.

All the historians agree that the arrest of Jesus took place in the Garden of Gethsemane at a late hour on the evening immediately preceding the day of the Crucifixion, and there is strong justification for believing that it could not possibly have been earlier than eleven-thirty.

This estimate is based upon the amount of time required by the recorded events between the breaking up of the supper party, probably in a house in the Upper City, and the arrival of the armed band in the garden at the foot of Olivet. There are three things which point irresistibly to the hour being late:

1. The disciples were manifestly tired, and even the sturdy fisherman Peter, accustomed to lonely vigils on the deep, could not keep awake.
2. Both St. Matthew and St. Mark refer to three separate periods of slumber, broken by the periodical return of Christ from His prolonged communing under the neighbouring trees.
3. The fact that it was quite dark, and that owing to the use of torches, Christ was able to discern the approach of the arrest party a considerable distance off (see St.

Mark xiv. 42: 'Arise, let us be going: behold, he that
betrayeth me is at hand.').

No one can read the records of this extraordinary episode
without realizing that this particular sojourn in the
garden was different from any of those previous visits to
the same spot hinted at by St. John. These men were being
held there by the will of Christ long after the time when
they would ordinarily have been in their beds at Bethany.
They were waiting at His bidding for something for
which He also was waiting, and which was an un-
conscionably long time in coming. Assuming the supper
to have been over at nine-thirty and the Garden itself
reached so early as 10 p.m., the arrest could hardly have
been effected much before eleven-thirty. This fixes for us
with some certainty the hour of the preliminary trial.

It is generally agreed by archaeologists and students of
the topography of ancient Jerusalem that an old flight of
steps descended from the Upper City to the gate leading
to the pool of Siloam at the south-eastern angle of the City
wall. It is mentioned by Nehemiah (Chap. iii. 15): 'The
stairs that go down from the city of David'; and again
(Chap. xii. 37): 'By the fountain gate, and straight before
them, they went up by the stairs of the city of David, at
the going up of the wall.'

There were thus two routes open to the arrest party.
One was to follow the course of the Kedron Valley to the
foot of these steps, and thence to the High Priest's house.
The other was to take the main Bethany road into the new
town and thence by the Tyropaean Valley to the Priestly
quarter. Even if tradition had not strongly indicated the
former, it is clear that to have conducted Jesus through
the populous quarter of the Lower City would not only
have been inexpedient, but would have necessitated a
detour by which valuable time would have been lost.

And in this strange nocturnal business time was a very important factor.

If, therefore, by some magic reversal of the centuries we could have stood at some vantage-point in old Jerusalem about midnight or shortly afterwards on that memorable 14 Nizan, we should probably have witnessed a small party of men leading a strangely unresisting figure through the darkness, along the rocky defile which skirted the precipitous eastern face of the Temple wall, up the historic causeway at the south-eastern angle of the city wall to the headquarters of His avowed and inveterate enemies.

How did it come about that the most distinguished Hebrew of His generation found Himself in this dangerous and menacing situation, at the dead of night, on the eve of one of the most solemn of the Jewish Festivals? What were the secret and hidden forces which precipitated His arrest? Why was this particular and highly inconvenient moment chosen? Above all, what was the gravamen of the charge which was brought against Him?

It will require very much more than this chapter to answer these questions, to which indeed the whole book is a very partial and inadequate reply. But there are two things which stand out very sharply from the records of this trial and which call for the closest study. The first is the peculiar nature of the only definite charge which was brought against Jesus. The second is the admission upon which His conviction was based.

Now it seems to me that we shall make a very grievous mistake if we assume (as has so often been done by Christian writers) that everything that the priests did that night was *ultra vires* and illegal. Of course, there are aspects of the affair which, on any reading of the case, must be considered definitely, and even flagrantly, to be at variance with the Jewish Law. That, I think, is conceded by every competent student of the Mischna and of Jewish institutions as they existed at the time.

It was illegal, for example, for the Temple Guard, acting officially as the instrument of the High Priest, to effect the arrest. That should have been left to the voluntary action of the witnesses. It was illegal to try a capital charge (Trial for Life) by night. Only 'trials for money' could be conducted after sunset. It was illegal, after the testimony of the witnesses had broken down, for the judges to cross-examine the Prisoner. They should have acquitted Him, and if the testimony given was demonstrably *false*, the witnesses should have been sentenced to death by stoning.

These things lie upon the surface of the situation. But beneath these flagrant instances of irregularity in the trial of Jesus, there runs a strong undercurrent of legality – an almost meticulous observance of certain minor points of the law – which is very illuminating and instructive to the impartial student of history.

This fact emerges very strikingly if we study the singular way in which the very ground of the accusation shifted during the course of the trial. As everyone who has attentively studied the records knows, there were in all three main charges brought against Jesus during the course of the successive phases of the trial. We may summarize them briefly as follows:

1. That He had threatened to destroy the Temple.
2. That He had claimed to be the Son of God.
3. That He had stirred up the people against Caesar.

The third of these charges can be dismissed from our consideration at once. It was not the real grievance of the Jews. It was framed solely for political ends. The Roman law took no cognizance of the offences for which Christ was condemned to death, yet without Pilate the death could not be consummated. It was absolutely necessary, therefore, to find a political charge to justify before the Roman procurator the extreme penalty which they had already tacitly imposed. They chose the charge of conspiracy against Caesar because it was the only kind of charge which would carry weight with Pontius Pilate, or indeed with any representative of the Roman Power. Even that almost failed, and would have failed completely, had the procuratorship been in stronger hands.

But, as I have said above, it does not matter what the ostensible charge before Pilate was. The thing we are concerned with very deeply is what the *real* charge of the Jews was against Christ. Directly we concentrate upon this we get an extraordinarily luminous view of what was behind the prosecution.

It must be remembered that, according to a long-established Hebrew custom, the accusers in a Jewish criminal trial were the witnesses. No other form of prosecution was legal, and the first clearly defined act in the midnight drama, after the Prisoner had been brought before the court, was the calling of witnesses, as the law demanded. Both St. Matthew and St. Mark are quite explicit upon this point.

St. Mark says: 'Many bare false witness against him.'

St. Matthew says: 'Many false witnesses came.'

And St. Mark affirms that the evidence of these witnesses did not 'agree together' and was therefore overthrown.

To those unfamiliar with the subtleties of Jewish jurispridence, and especially with the singular orientation of the law in favour of the prisoner, it may seem curious that, having been at considerable pains to secure witnesses for the prosecution, the court should have proceeded forthwith to *reject* the evidence. If the story of the witnesses was a deliberate fabrication, it should not have been very difficult to have harmonized it in advance, or, in the ancient phraseology, to have made it 'agree together'. The very fact that the Court did reject the testimony proves that in this fundamental matter of the witnesses even Caiaphas himself was under some compelling necessity to follow the traditional and characteristic Hebrew usage in a 'trial for life'.

What that usage was is described for us with great wealth of detail in the Mischna. There were three classes of testimony recognized by the law:

1. A vain testimony.
2. A standing testimony.
3. An adequate testimony.

Now there was a very practical distinction between these three classes of evidence. A 'vain testimony' was testimony obviously irrelevant or worthless, and immediately recognized by the judges as such. A 'standing testimony' was evidence of a more serious kind to be accepted provisionally, until confirmed or otherwise. An 'adequate testimony' was evidence in which the witnesses 'agreed together'. The least discordance between the evidence of witnesses' (says the distinguished Jewish writer, Salvador) 'was held to destroy its value.'

It is clear, therefore, that whatever may have been the subject-matter of the preliminary witnesses referred to by the two Evangelists, it did not get beyond the second and provisional stage. This can only mean that it was either demonstrably contrary to the experience and knowledge of the court, or it was invalidated on technical grounds. St. Mark's statement that it did not 'agree together' strongly indicates the latter.

But now comes a very curious thing. When this preliminary and unsatisfactory witness had been cleared away, two men came forward with a very definite and circumstantial piece of evidence.

St. Mark says:

> There stood up certain, and bare false witness against him, saying, We heard him say, I will destroy this temple that is made with hands, and in three days I will build another made without hands.

St. Matthew, who in this case is probably not quoting St. Mark, but drawing upon another ancient source, confirms it by saying:

> But afterward came two, and said, This man said, I am able to destroy the temple of God and to build it in three days.

Whatever else took place, therefore, on that memorable night, it seems certain that two men came forward and, with the torchlight falling full on the face of Christ, accused Him of having used words similar to these. That is a very important fact, and I will ask the reader to keep it in mind for a few moments.

Now the thing of immediate importance is to know whether these men were deliberately inventing the charge or were merely perverting for their own purpose an actual and somewhat similar saying of Christ. Even if no other data were available, I should personally hesitate to believe that so definite and circumstantial a statement was a pure invention. It is a much more deadly thing to distort what a man has said in the hearing of others than to lie deliberately about him. The distortion will elicit uproarious support from overwrought and angry men.

Only the most brazen will voice approval of a deliberate
and calculated lie. It always has been so, and we can be
reasonably sure that it was so in this case. These men had
heard Christ make a resounding statement in the Temple
courts, and there was no more deadly thing which they
could do than to give a distorted and misleading version
of it at His trial.

But there is another, and, to me, a very conclusive
reason why we may regard the testimony of these
witnesses as a reflex of something which Christ Himself
actually said on some public occasion. Both men declared
that they had heard the Prisoner use certain words
which, if substantiated, involved the double offence of
sorcery and sacrilege. The penalty for sorcery was death.
The penalty for sacrilege was stoning and exposure of the
body. From the standpoint of the enemies of Jesus a more
fatal charge could hardly have been laid to His account.
Yet still the testimony was overthrown.

Now why was that? There must be a satisfactory and
historical explanation. If the testimony of these two men
had been an absolute invention; if it had originated in the
scheming brain of Caiaphas, and the witnesses had, so to
say, been 'put up' to play their part, there would surely
have been no bungling of the affair in this naive and
exasperating way. After all, the witnesses had only a few
words to say, and the most elementary sort of prudence
should have secured their agreement in advance. The
case against Christ ought to have gone swiftly and
triumphantly to a conviction.

But we do not find that kind of situation at all. We find
a situation in which the Court, despite the illegality of its
sitting at this very late hour, wasted a great deal of
precious time upon a judicial process which carried it
nowhere. At the end of all this elaborate hearing of
witnesses Jesus Christ was virtually an unaccused, and

certainly an unconvicted man. The entire proceedings threatened to breakdown upon a vital point of Jewish Law.

Two things emerge from this unquestionably historic fact. In the first place Caiaphas was clearly not all-powerful to work his will in that assembly. There were evidently very strong influences in the Council Chamber in favour of a rigorous observance of the law, particularly in the crucial matter of the witnesses. It must always be remembered that the judgment of this tribunal was not final. Whatever these men did that night had to pass muster the next morning before the Great Sanhedrin in plenary sitting. There had apparently been trouble once before when Nicodemus, a member of that body, had protested against condemnation without a fair hearing. They could justify the illegality of the night hearing of the case on the ground of high political necessity, and the near approach of the Feast. But any serious flaw in the accusation might easily have led to the compulsory release of the Prisoner at a moment when immense multitudes would unquestionably have flocked to His side.

The very fact, too, that the testimony was being sifted so rigorously implies a corresponding cautiousness of statement by the witnesses themselves. Under the Jewish system of jurisprudence, weighted as it undoubtedly was to lean in favour of the accused, it was a very dangerous thing to be a witness in a 'trial for life'. The penalty for uttering a false testimony was death. Hence the number of these trials was few.

But the really impressive inference from all these singular proceedings is surely this: If the testimony was *not* preconcerted; if its disagreement both surprised and exasperated the high priest, it is clear that it was at least *bona-fide* testimony, and bore some definite relation to the facts. Thus, even if the writer of St. John's Gospel had not preserved for us what we may call the 'official' version of what took place in the Temple courts, we should be compelled to believe that Jesus did upon some historical occasion use some words closely resembling those with which He was charged.

What was the historic utterance which lay behind this charge? What did Jesus really say to give rise to these circumstantial statements? There are three versions from which we may choose. According to St. Mark's 'witness' Jesus deliberately threatened to destroy the Temple and to replace it magically in three days. The words are very explicit:

> I will destroy this temple that is made with hands, and in three days I will build another made without hands.

St. Matthew's witness modifies and softens the accusation considerably. The suggestion of the magical replacement of the Temple is still there, but Christ is represented as only claiming the *power* to do this:

> This man said, I am able to destroy the temple of God, and to build it in three days.

Can we, in the absence of a more authentic version of what the original utterance was, accept either of these statements as the true one? Surely we cannot without doing violence to the whole Synoptic impression of the historic Jesus. For consider their import. Jesus is made to say that, of His own power and volition, He could pull down the Temple of Herod, or cause it to fall down, or disappear, and replace it by another. Such a claim could, of course, only be validated by the exercise of super-normal or magical powers beyond anything ever asserted of Christ, and beyond the wildest dreams of the most deluded disciple of Eastern necromancy. Indeed, we may say that no really sane person, especially one of the spiritual and moral category to which Christ belongs, would make a statement of this particular sort.

We can imagine some fanatical and half-witted person, whose whole mentality bordered on the insane, throwing out this preposterous boast in a sudden access of frenzy, knowing full well that he would never be called upon to justify it. But the Prisoner in this trial does not come within that definition. He does not come within a thousand miles of it. In all His story there is no trace of those characteristics which are the hall-mark of the unstable mind. On the other hand, there are many indications of that high sanity which accompanies a firmly disciplined mind. He seems to have been supremely a lover of truth and sincerity, and that inner humility which is man's greatest claim to kinship with God; He was a great hater of shams and hypocrisies and futile boasts. Moreover, He was a somewhat shy and intensely sensitive man. No one with an eye for historic truth, flashing out of the ancient pages of His record, can fail to see what happened when they brought to Him the woman taken in adultery. He *blushed,* and He stooped to write in the sand that He might cover His momentary confusion and regain the moral poise which a public situation attended with peculiarly indelicate and disgusting elements demanded. There, if anywhere, you have a glimpse of the real Jesus of history. It rings true with the memorable moral sayings recorded of Him. But it does not ring true with this grotesque and overweening boast.

The version of two witnesses, therefore, must at least be held suspect until we have corroborative testimony of the most emphatic kind. But the evidence at our disposal points in quite a different direction. According to St. John, what Jesus really did say was: 'Destroy this temple and in three days I will raise it up.' And the writer adds parenthetically: 'But he spake of the temple of his body.'

Of course, no serious student of this problem will deny for a moment that this is a difficult saying. It is difficult whatever interpretation is put upon it. But if we are to decide between three divergent and contradictory readings, I am bound to say that there is one thing which impresses me profoundly – the fact that *the words 'in three days' are found in them all.* I do not think that the immense weight of that circumstance has been fully realized.

In ordinary life, when confronted with several divergent accounts of a given happening, it is a sound and consistent rule to examine first the points upon which the narrators are agreed. The presumption that such points of agreement represent something solid and original is very strong. Particularly is this the case when the witnesses come, as it were, from opposite camps, and are in marked disagreement upon other essential features of the case.

Now the peculiarity of the phrase 'in three days' lies in the fact that it occurs very rarely in the recorded teaching of Christ, and then only in circumstances which have seemed to many critics to present grave doubts as to the authenticity of the passages in question. Take, for example, the three outstanding instances which occur in the Gospel of St. Mark:

> *Mark viii.* 31: And he began to teach them, that the Son of man must suffer many things, and be rejected by the elders, and the chief priests, and the scribes, and be killed, and after three days rise again.
> *Mark ix.* 31: For he taught his disciples, and said unto them, The Son of man is delivered up into the hands of men, and they shall kill him; and when he is killed, after three days he shall rise again.

Mark x. 33: Behold, we go up to Jerusalem; and the Son of man shall be delivered unto the chief priests and the scribes; and they shall condemn him to death, and shall deliver him unto the Gentiles: and they shall mock him, and shall spit upon him, and shall scourge him, and shall kill him; and after three days he shall rise again.

The modern reader, coming to these passages with a certain instinctive reluctance to accept anything which transcends the field of normal experience is inclined to say: 'I can understand Jesus predicting His own death. He must have foreseen what was the probable outcome of the ever widening gap between Himself and the priests, and I think it is not unlikely that He may have prepared the disciples privately for the event. But surely these direct references to His rising from the dead can only have been written after His death and are not an integral part of the original utterances.'

Let us admit frankly that it does look like that at first sight. And yet when we come to examine closely the minutes of this trial with all its primitive marks of authenticity; its meticulous and, in the end, fruitless hearing of hostile witnesses; we make the startling discovery that these very words ('in three days') which reason asserts *could never have been uttered by Christ,* are precisely the words which according to all the witnesses formed the pith and core of the fatal and historic sentence with which He was charged. It would have been a strange coincidence indeed if the one sentence chosen by the enemies of Christ upon which to base the most deadly charge they could bring against Him found no counterpart or parallel whatever in all the varied teaching of the two preceding years.

What, then, do we find? We find the Prisoner accused of making a claim so fantastic and absurd that, even if His judges had not rejected the testimony, we should have had to receive it with the gravest possible doubt. Yet from the very texture of the circumstances there seems to emerge the fact that what He probably did say was more extraordinary still.

He said in effect: 'If you kill me I will rise again from the grave.' I see no escape from the logic of that conclusion. We may hold that He was mistaken; that He was held by some strange mental obsession which periodically flashed out in His public utterance. But that He said this singular and almost unbelievable thing seems to me to be very nearly beyond the possibility of doubt.

But we have still to consider the other outstanding feature of this remarkable trial. Jesus of Nazareth was condemned to death, not upon the statements of His accusers, but upon an admission extorted from Him under oath.

It is clear that after the hearing of the witnesses, and the final rejection of their testimony, the whole conduct of the case began to take an unquestionably illegal form. The illegality consisted in the President of the Court attempting to supply, by direct questioning of the Prisoner, the necessary grounds for a conviction which the witnesses themselves had been unable to produce.

This was, of course, directly contrary both to the letter and the spirit of the elaborate judicial code by which the Jewish Law sought to protect the life of the citizen. The power of accusation in a Hebrew 'trial for life' was vested solely in the witnesses. It was their business to effect the arrest and to bring the accused man to the court. It was the duty of the court to protect the interests of the Prisoner in every possible way, while seeking to arrive at a just and impartial judgment on the evidence submitted.

That this judicial protection was not extended to the Prisoner in the present case is clear from even a superficial reading of the narrative. It comes out in the tone of marked exasperation with which the High Priest addressed the Prisoner when the last of the long line of testimonies had broken down.

Answerest thou nothing? What is it which these witness against thee?

In itself this question was perhaps not objectionable. As an accused man Christ undoubtedly had the right to bring forward any facts or explanations in His defence. Hitherto He had maintained complete silence. It was appropriate that He should be asked if He had anything to say bearing on the evidence. It is the unveiled hostility to the Prisoner which is so significant, and which instinctively warns us of what is to follow. For, in the next moment, the High Priest seems to have thrown all pretence at legality to the winds.

Standing in his place, in the centre of the tribunal, Caiaphas applied to Christ the most solemn form of oath known to the Hebrew Constitution, the famous Oath of the Testimony. 'I adjure thee by the living God' (Matthew xxvi. 63). To this, Christ, as a pious and law-abiding Jew, had no alternative but to answer.

If (says the Mischna) one shall say, I adjure you by the Almighty, by Sabaoth, by the Gracious and Merciful, by the Long-suffering, by the Compassionate, or by any of the Divine titles, behold they are bound to answer.

Stripped of the peculiar phraseology with which the Hebrew mind of the period invested the conception of the Messiah, the question which Caiaphas, the High Priest, put to Jesus was a direct and simple one:

Art thou the Christ? Dost thou claim to be He that shall come?

The reply of the Prisoner was not less direct. Here are the three versions:

I am (Mark xiv. 62).
Thou hast said (Matthew xxvi. 64).
Ye say that I am (Luke xxii. 70).

As Mr. Baring Gould has pointed out, these answers are really identical. The formulae 'Thou hast said' or 'Ye say that I am', which to modern ears sound evasive, had no such connotation to the contemporary Jewish mind. 'Thou sayest' was the traditional form in which a cultivated Jew replied to a question of grave or sad import. Courtesy forbade a direct 'yes' or 'no'.

Christ therefore said this very considerable thing with great definiteness and emphasis. The satisfaction of Caiaphas at obtaining by a single stroke this tremendous and (from the Prisoner's standpoint) very dangerous confession is obvious. One can almost hear the ring of triumph in his voice as he swung round upon the assembled rabbis and exclaimed :

What further need have we of witnesses? Ye have heard the blasphemy: what think ye?

Now to the student whose mind is alert for what I may call the *submerged* facts of the story, this sudden rising of the case to its dramatic climax is full of interest.

Why did the trial suddenly take this pronouncedly un-constitutional form at a relatively late hour in the proceedings, after much valuable time had been occu-pied in sifting the evidence of the witnesses? If the compulsory affirmation of the Prisoner was sufficient to secure conviction, why were the witnesses heard at all?

The answer to these questions lies undoubtedly in the peculiar nature of the tactical and judicial problem which confronted Caiaphas. That the powerful Sadducean family to which the High Priest belonged had fully determined to get Jesus out of the way is obvious, and nothing but the death penalty would satisfy them. Yet, strangely enough, even an indisputably proven case of blasphemy or sorcery was not sufficient. Caiaphas had to look beyond the purists of the Great Sanhedrin and the provisions of the Mosaic Law to that far more formidable barrier, the power and tolerance of Rome.

None knew better than Caiaphas what were the personal and political consequences of the coming of the real Messiah in the flesh. That it involved some definite kind of Kingship, with Jerusalem and the Holy Places as its Court, is obvious. It involved, further, an immediate and sanguinary clash with the Roman garrisons throughout the land. It meant a vast uprising of the people, and the certainty of a punitive expedition, led, by a Roman leader of resource, such as that which forty years later laid the city in ruins.

All these things belong to the broad outlines of a situation which was as inevitable as that night follows day. These facts could not have escaped the penetrating eyes of those responsible for the maintenance of the hard-won Jewish privileges under the Roman occupation. Caiaphas, as the acting High Priest, made an exceedingly acute observation in political statecraft when he said:

> It is expedient for you that one man should die for the people, and that the whole nation perish not (John xi. 50).

But the personal consequences to Caiaphas and his family were hardly less distasteful. We do not know what changes in the Constitution of the Great Sanhedrin would have taken place under a truly Messianic regime. They would probably have been very considerable. But one thing is certain: the supreme ascendancy of the High Priest, as the arbiter of the national fortunes, would have suffered eclipse. Whatever aspects of its ancient and historic form the Hebrew Constitution might have retained, the real Dynast would have been the Messiah. As the national Deliverer and the supreme Representative of the God of Israel, His right to impose policy and to direct events would have been final and absolute. The prospect of the Nazarene Carpenter stepping into this unique and unparalleled seat of national power must have been profoundly disturbing to certain men (and women) who had an unquestioned interest in the maintenance of the *status quo*.

The problem, therefore, was to bring a conclusive case which was not only proof against possible criticism by the Seventy-one, but which also gave indisputable grounds for action under the Roman law.

In the search for this formula many witnesses were apparently examined and their testimony rejected as insufficient. Then came two witnesses with what seemed to be a particularly promising case. It involved two offences, each punishable by death under the Hebrew Code. Yet here again the same fatal weakness disclosed itself. It might pass the Sanhedrin, but would it pass the Roman Procurator? Most assuredly it would not. Something more serious than this apparently idle threat to destroy and rebuild the Temple would be necessary to secure the assent of Pilate to a penalty which had been expressly removed by Caesar from sectarian hands.

The whole prosecution was thus obviously on the point of breaking down when the alert brain of Caiaphas conceived an expedient for saving the situation. It was illegal; but it was the last desperate throw of a man pushed to the very edge of endurance by the miscarriage of his plans. He applied the Oath of the Testimony, to which even silence itself was an unforgivable offence. It succeeded probably beyond his dreams, because in that fearless reply, 'I am', there flashed out the long-sought base of the deadliest of all charges before the Roman Procurator.

Caesar might be indifferent to the somewhat eccentric utterances of an itinerant preacher. He could not be indifferent to a claimant for a throne. In the hush of the Court, as the solemn words of the affirmation fell from the Prisoner's lips, certain other words were probably already forming in the mind of Caiaphas: 'If thou lettest this man go, thou art not Caesar's friend.'

Study Questions

1 *The author deals painstakingly with the details of Jesus' trial. What is your initial response to Morison's presentation? What value is there in knowing the details?*

2 *Imagine a non-Christian asking you the following question: 'How did it come about that the most distinguished Hebrews of his generation found himself in this dangerous and menacing situation, at the dead of night, on the eve of one of the most solemn of the Jewish Festivals?' How would you answer?*

3 *Reread Mark 14: 53-65 taking note of the scene where the Oath of the Testimony was invoked. What do we learn about Caiaphas from this question and about Jesus from his reply? Why do you think God allowed Jesus' own oath to condemn him to death?*

4   *Why were the religious leaders so vehement in their opposition of Jesus? Can you think of examples where the religious establishment and even we as individuals oppose Jesus today?*

5   *The physical suffering of Jesus begins in Mark 14:65 but look for example in Mark 14:32–52, 66–72 for the other ways he must have been suffering. In what similar ways do we cause Jesus to suffer? If it is appropriate, in twos discuss and pray together how in your particular situation you could bring Jesus pleasure instead of pain this Lent.*

10. 'Stayin' Ready 'til Quittin' Time'

by Charles Swindoll

After I graduated from high school, I worked in a machine shop in Houston's industrial district for four-and-a-half years. I was not only learning the machinist trade as an apprentice, I was also going to night school at the University of Houston. My father was from the old school of thought; he believed I should not only get a good education but also learn a trade so I would have something to fall back on if some career I followed ever fell through. I followed his advice and have never regretted it.

I have many great memories of those years in that machine shop. I learned a lot of valuable lessons while working with my hands − one of them being a true appreciation for the blue-collar world. I have no trouble understanding what that life is like, its pressures and frustrations as well as its benefits and feelings of accomplishment.

I often recall several unforgettable characters I met during those days. What fun we had together! One of them was a fellow I'll call Tex. He and I worked alongside each other on second shift for several months.

Tex had spent most of his adult life operating a turret lathe in the same shop. He was your typical machinist. He wore a little grey-and-white striped cap – always greasy – and overalls that needed an oil change. And, of course, he chewed tobacco, which meant he spit a lot. He would keep his tobacco pouch open in his right hip pocket; and as he ran his lathe, he would reach back, grab a fistful of that stringy stuff, cram it into his mouth, then chew on it for an hour or so. That entire procedure occurred without his eyes ever leaving his work on the lathe. Tex would easily chew his way through several pouches a week.

One hot, sticky night as I was working behind Tex on a similar lathe, I noticed that a Texas-size cricket hopped unassumingly through the door onto the floor of our shop. As I studied the little critter, I noticed that the colour of the cricket was almost identical to the colour of the tobacco in Tex's pouch. So, without Tex knowing it, I strolled over and stepped on Jiminy, quickly putting him out of his misery. I then plucked the head off the little guy, reached over and placed him very gently on the top of the open tobacco pouch sticking out of Tex's pocket. I then quietly strolled back to my lathe and waited … and watched.

After a while he needed to replenish his chaw, so he reached back and grabbed a fresh fistful. In went the cricket along with a jaw full of tobacco. To this day Tex has no idea what he chewed that night. I can still remember watching him spit wings and legs and body parts for the next hour or so. It was hilarious!

When you work in a machine shop, your life revolves around a whistle. After punching the clock when you arrive, your work begins with a whistle. As lunchtime arrives, it is announced by the same shrill sound. When your shift ends, there is yet another blast.

Shoptalk for that final whistle is 'quittin' time.'

Tex had worked so long in a machine shop, he had kind of an invisible sensor down inside. He seldom had a look at the clock. Somehow he always knew when it was getting close to that last whistle. I cannot recall his ever being caught short. Without fail, Tex was all washed up and ready to punch out a couple of minutes before the whistle blew.

On one occasion I said to him, 'Well, Tex, it's about time to start gettin' ready for quittin' time.'

I will never forget his response. In that slow Texas drawl, he said, 'Listen, boy … I stay ready to keep from gettin' ready for quittin' time.' It was his way of saying, 'That final whistle won't ever catch me unaware.'

Many long years have passed since I worked with Tex, but his answer has stuck in my mind when I think of that last sound before our Lord comes back. It won't be from a whistle in a machine shop, but with other sounds far more earsplitting. In fact Scripture says,

> The Lord Himself will descend from heaven with a **shout** … (1 Thessalonians 4: 16).

The word means 'an outcry.' I don't know if it will be the Lord Himself or someone near Him, but there will be a loud outcry from heaven. And that's not all. There will also be –

> … the voice of the archangel, and with the trumpet of God (v. 16).

And then –

> … the dead in Christ shall rise first. Then we who are alive and remain shall be caught up together with them in the clouds to meet the Lord in the air, and thus we shall always be with the

Lord. Therefore comfort one another with these words (1 Thessalonians 4:16–17).

Are you 'stayin' ready 'til quittin' time'? There are times I wonder how many will be caught off guard. Do thoughts ever come to your mind, as you are busily engaged in your daily grind, like, 'Say, it may happen today. It could be right after supper.'? Or, 'He may return before bedtime tonight.' Let me tell you when most of us think such a thought: when we have to pay our taxes! That's when we all wish He would come quickly. But, seriously, does it ever flash through your head, 'Today could be my last day on earth. He could split the heavens today and shout "It's quittin' time!"'?

Some folks would have to admit that thought never crosses their minds I mean, *never*, even though while He was still on earth, our Lord gave numerous predictions about His coming back.

A few predictions from Jesus' life

Let's look at several. I've chosen one from each of the four Gospels.

Periodically, during the ministry of Christ, He spoke of this. Each time He mentioned His certain return, His words seemed like a wake-up call in the early morning hours.

Therefore be on the alert, for you do not know which day your Lord is coming. But be sure of this, that if the head of the house had known at what time of the night the thief was coming, he would have been on the alert and would not have allowed his house to be broken into (Matthew 24:42–43).

How practical! If you have ever been gone overnight and had your home broken into by a burglar, or if your place of business has ever been robbed in the middle of the night, you know that the thief was successful because his entrance was unexpected and his exit undetected. That's Jesus' point here. 'My coming will be like a thief in the night. When you least expect it, I'll come.' He then applies this to His return:

> For this reason you be ready too; for the Son of Man is coming at an hour when you do not think He will (v. 44).

I once read about an armoured car that was left un-attended for less than five minutes. It had over a million dollars in it. During those unattended moments, thieves came and robbed it. They knew just when to come and how to leave so that no one had any idea they were there – until it was too late.

We find similar words about the same event in Mark's Gospel. Again, Jesus is speaking:

> Take heed, keep on the alert; for you do not know when the appointed time is. It is like a man, away on a journey, who upon leaving his house and putting his slaves in charge, assigning to each one his task, also commanded the doorkeeper to stay on the alert. Therefore, be on the alert – for you do not know when the master of the house is coming, whether in the evening, at midnight, at cockcrowing, or in the morning – lest he come suddenly and find you asleep. And what I say to you I say to all, 'Be on the alert!' (13:33-37)

You and I are intrigued with His reference to 'cock-crowing', aren't we? It calls for an explanation. Our nights are not divided as they were in Jesus' time. First-century nights were divided into watches – four

three-hour watches, to be exact. The first watch began at
sundown, around 6:00 p.m., and ended at 9:00 p.m. The
second watch continued from 9:00 p.m. until 12:00
midnight. And the third watch occurred from 12:00
midnight to 3:00 in the morning.

There was a familiar Latin term used to describe the
end of the third watch, *gallicinium*. It meant 'cock-
crowing.' I suppose the name was derived from some
early-rising rooster that would stretch his neck and
sound his first call around three in the morning. Christ
could come then! Or, says our Lord, He may come at
dawn, in the misty morning hour around sunrise. The
point is: *anytime*.

Dr. Luke records similar words. The more we read
these repeated words of Jesus, the more assured we
become: Not only is He coming back ... we must be ready.

> *Be on guard, that your hearts may not be weighted down with*
> *dissipation and drunkenness and the worries of life, and that day*
> *come on you like a trap* (Luke 21:34).

How different! Matthew used the analogy of a thief, but
now Luke mentions a trap. If you are trapped in an
embarrassing setting, full of worry, or in a drunken state
or a dissipating lifestyle – as some people will be – you
won't be ready for quittin' time. His warning is clear:
Don't be caught short lest you be trapped at His coming.

> *For it will come upon all those who dwell on the face of all the*
> *earth. But keep on the alert at all times, praying in order that you*
> *may have strength to escape all these things that are about to take*
> *place, and to stand before the Son of Man* (vv. 35–36).

Many years later, at the end of the first century, John
recorded his observations and thoughts. Among John's

most significant contributions were his writings of the Upper Room discourse. Jesus is with His Twelve the night before He is taken under arrest and goes to the cross. While there, He abruptly unveils the truth of His impending death. It catches the disciples off guard. They became visibly shaken, and understandably so. Had we been among His disciples, we, too, would have expected Him to live forever, establish His kingdom, and take us with Him as He became the King of kings and Lord of lords, ruling over the whole earth.

But suddenly He introduces a change in the game plan – the cross. Full of turmoil, doubt, and fear, the disciples stared in stunned amazement as He spoke of His imminent death. That explains why He said what He did to them regarding His return.

> *Let not your heart be troubled; believe in God, believe also in Me. In My Father's house are many dwelling places; if it were not so, I would have told you; for I go to prepare a place for you. And if I go and prepare a place for you, I will come again, and receive you to Myself; that where I am, there you may be also* (John 14:1-3).

To those anxious disciples He gave an unconditional promise. He doesn't say, 'If you're expecting Me, I'll come back.' He doesn't even say, 'If you're walking with Me, I'll come back.' No, His promise is absolutely un-conditional. 'I am going to prepare a place ... I will return ... I will receive you ... you will be with Me.' His return was no guesswork ... it would occur!

No doubt, they wondered what to expect in the meanwhile. Within minutes He covered that base.

> *These things I have spoken to you, that in Me you may have peace. In the world you have tribulation, but take courage; I have overcome the world* (John 16:33).

'I have left heaven. I have begun My ministry on this earth. I have been sustained by God's power. I will soon complete My mission. I must go to the cross to pay the penalty for sins. I will come out of the grave victorious. I will ascend to the Father. And I will come again at His appointed time.' In the meantime, He challenged them to be alert. 'Stay ready 'til quittin' time.' While awaiting His return, they were sure to face affliction and tribulation.

Since the world is going to make times hard for us, how can we live courageously, knowing that He has overcome the world? What are we in the church to do? Clearly, Christ is going to return. Our question is this: How can we best 'stay ready 'til quittin' time'?

Specific principles from Paul's pen

Turn again to those last words Paul wrote in the second letter to Timothy. He penned these words a little past A.D. 60. He has come to the end of his life, which prompts him to describe life at the end of time. Paul pulls no punches as he writes his friend Timothy and says, 'We're in for difficult times ... savage, in fact.' How can we stay ready for the finale? How can we be sure that the curtain's closing will not take us by surprise or find us finishing poorly? What are we to do?

There are four principles to follow. They are set forth in the third and fourth chapters of 2 Timothy. The first principle: *Follow the model of the faithful.*

> *But you followed my teaching, conduct, purpose and faith, patience, love, perseverance, persecutions, and sufferings, such as happened to me at Antioch, at Iconium and at Lystra; what persecutions I endured, and out of them all the Lord delivered me! And indeed, all who desire to live godly lives in Christ Jesus will be persecuted* (2 Timothy 3:10–12).

There is nothing more encouraging or more motivating than a model to keep us going.

I don't know if you've read of the five-hundred-mile dogsled race over a part of Minnesota. Have you kept up on that? The same lady who won in 1987 also won in 1988. We're talking a pioneer woman. She pressed on through bitter cold, the howling winds of a blizzard, dark nights, and exhausting days, as her well-trained huskies pulled her sled over those hundreds of miles from the start to the finish of the race. The dogs were fitted with little socks over their paws since the ice resembles sandpaper after so many miles. It can literally rip the pads off their feet. Though strong and in great condition, the struggling animals with those little socks on their feet barked, pulled, and pressed on in spite of the odds.

After the race she was interviewed and asked, 'How did you do it?'

'Well' she said, 'I just remembered that others have done it before me, so I can do it, too.'

If that wasn't enough, when I shared that story recently, I had a fellow say to me, 'Did you know there is an eleven-hundred-mile race from Anchorage to Nome?' He then informed me that the same woman, Susan Butcher, has won that race three times in a row! Is that unbelievable? Ten to twelve days in the middle of nowhere. Maddening monotony. Strain beyond belief. How does she do it? I can tell you part of her answer ... she remembers someone else did it before her. That assures her that she can do it too.

The same works today. By following the model of those who have gone before us, we can do more than survive. We can overcome! That is how composers of music stay at the task of writing music. That is how people exist through torturous conditions as prisoners of war. That is how surgeons continue to push on through the night hours in emergency surgery. That is how athletes set new records. There have been models who have done it before.

The same works in the spiritual life. That is why Paul tells Timothy to follow the model of his faithful mother and grandmother ... and Paul's own example as well.

What a rich heritage! Timothy had deep roots to sustain him through dry and unfruitful days.

The second principle: *Return to the truth of your past.* As you follow the model of the faithful, go back to the things you learned from your mother, the truth you gleaned from your grandmother, and your early years at the feet of a mentor in the classroom. Go back to those truths that stabilized you when you put down your spiritual roots.

I spent a few hours in Chicago several years ago, recording an interview with *Leadership* magazine. There were four of us who had been invited from various sections of the country to be interviewed. I'll never forget a comment from one of the men who holds a responsible position in a sizable denomination. He has his finger on the pulse of the church at large. He said something like this:

> We have discovered that those who make the best church leaders, those who hold important and responsible positions over vast numbers of people, are almost without exception people who have deep, longstanding roots in the faith. Very few of them were saved at, say, age 35 or 40, and are now leading a large segment of God's family. Almost without exception, those who have been promoted to places of great responsibility can look back to godly parents and even grandparents who walked with God. And from them they learned, even from early childhood, the value of the church, the significance of the Scriptures.

Don't misread that statement. It doesn't mean if you were saved later in life you will never be given a place of great responsibility. As Christians, all of us have great responsibilities. It's just interesting that the majority of those who are in high-profile leadership positions in the church today heard the truth early in life. They had solid Christian roots. If that was your experience, it is a great time to give thanks for the kind of faith you drew from them.

And notice in verse 15 that he has in mind,

> *... the sacred writings which are able to give you wisdom ...*

What are the sacred writings? The next verse gives the answer:

> *All Scripture is inspired by God ... (v. 16).*

Beautiful word – inspired. *Theos* (God), plus *pneuma* (breath) – *theopneustos* is the Greek word ... 'God-breathed.' All Scripture it its original form has been breathed out by God so that a writer, under the controlling power of the Spirit of God, wrote the Scriptures precisely as God would have written them. He did this without error, down to the very terms used, including the order of the terms in which they were written, with the result that God's very word was miraculously recorded. "All of that was 'God-breathed' Timothy."

But that isn't where it ends. It has been preserved in the pages of our Bibles so that as a result of reading and absorbing the Scriptures, we find them

> *... profitable for teaching, for reproof, for correction, for training in righteousness ... (v. 16).*

Isn't that a grand set of benefits? As important as it may be, great parenting is not an absolute prerequisite for spiritual growth or involvement in church leadership. God has given each of us the Bible in our tongue, with the promise that it is profitable for teaching, for reproof, for correction and for training in righteousness. Each one of us has the potential to become, like Timothy, a person who is adequate, mature, equipped for every good work. God's truth has been deposited into our reservoir. All this explains how Paul can say to his friend Timothy, 'In the hard times draw upon the Scriptures.'

Unfortunately, there is a chapter break in our Bibles between 2 Timothy 3:17 and 2 Timothy 4:1 which interrupts the flow of thought. Ignore it. Simply consider the new chapter as a continuation of the same theme.

> *I solemnly charge you in the presence of God and of Christ Jesus, who is to judge the living and the dead, and by His appearing and kingdom* (v. 1).

As he mentions our Lord's judging the living and the dead, Paul is reminding Timothy of Christ's return. 'Quittin' time' is a sure fact. 'Until He comes back, Timothy …'

> *Preach the word; be ready in season and out of season; reprove, rebuke, exhort, with great patience and instruction* (v. 2).

This statement brings us to the third 'survival' principle: *Proclaim the message of Christ.* Timothy has been called to be a preacher. It makes sense that he proclaimed Christ. You may not be a preacher, but the principle *still* applies. In light of these difficult days, all of us must heed the same command.

As I think about Paul's instruction, I find three ingredients. First, I find *urgency*. Be ready. 'Stay ready to keep from gettin' ready!' Be ready with the right message at all times.

Second, I find *consistency*. 'Be ready in season and out of season' Let's make a list.

- When it is convenient. When it is inconvenient.
- When others are open. When others are closed.
- When you're feeling good or you're feeling poorly.
- Whether you're young or old.
- Whether early or late.
- Whether it is cold and windy or hot and humid.
- Whether you're in public or private, at home or in a strange place.
- When you're appreciated or when you're resented.
- When you're asked about it or when you're not asked about it.

In season, out of season ... that's Paul's way of saying that the secret is consistency. What an effective force are those who know the truth and consistently live it out and share it. When we do, the Scriptures become absorbed into our very being.

Spurgeon put it this way:

> It is blessed to eat into the very soul of the Bible, until, at last, you come to talk in scriptural language, and your spirit is flavoured with the words of the Lord, so that your blood is Bibline and the very essence of the Bible flows from you.

Third, I find *simplicity*. Isn't it beautiful? There is nothing sophisticated about Paul's exhortation. No theories, no complex opinions. 'Just take the body of truth that I have given and declare it. Since you have the Scriptures, you have all the groceries you need for folks who are hungry.' God's Word contains sufficient comfort, hope, and encouragement to help the lonely and the hurting. Our need is to keep it simple. There is something quietly motivating about simplicity.

In one of my earlier books I cited a simple note emerging from the black and brutal days of the Civil War. The communication came from a battle-weary President Lincoln to his general, Ulysses S. Grant. Only three lines, yet it was the written missile that ended the war. The date and the time appeared at the top:

April 7, 1865
11o'clock a.m.

General Sheridan says, 'If the thing is pressed, I think that Lee will surrender.' Let the thing be pressed.

A. Lincoln

Grant got the message, and acted upon it. He pressed it. Two days later at Appomattox courthouse, Robert E. Lee surrendered. The thing was pressed, and the bloodiest war in American history ended. Simplicity is indeed powerful.

You want to stay ready 'til quittin' time?

• Follow the model of the faithful
• Return to the truth of your past.
• Proclaim the message of Christ

There is a final principle: *Maintain an exemplary life.*

> *For the time will come when they will not endure sound doctrine; but wanting to have their ears tickled, they will accumulate for*

themselves teachers in accordance to their own desires; and will turn away their ears from the truth, and will turn aside to myths. But you, be sober in all things, endure hardship, do the work of an evangelist, fulfil your ministry (vv. 3–5).

There will always be teachers who tickle people's fancy, telling them what they want to hear rather than what they *ought* to hear. Count on it – the closer we get to the Saviour's return, the more these ear-ticklers will proliferate. How are we to counteract that?

The answer appears in four staccato commands in verse 5:

- Be sober in all things.
- Endure hardship.
- Do the work of an evangelist.
- Fulfil your ministry.

Because people are unstable and forever on a search for cute fads and clever novelties, we are to steer clear of all that nonsense, staying calm and steady. Once again, John Stott's words are worth repeating:

> When men and women get intoxicated with heady heresies and sparkling novelties [we] must keep calm and sane.

Want a tip for finding the right church? Look for the ministry that is calm and sane. Stay away from those who highlight all the flash-in-the-pan fads, the cutesy, the clever.

And when the going gets rougher, 'endure hardship.' In today's terms, gut it out. Stay at it. But don't get sour and cranky. Just keep on presenting Christ. Realising that the phony and the false will be on the increase, live the truth, walk your talk. By doing that you 'fulfil your ministry.'

Timeless facts that maintain our readiness

> *For I am already being poured out as a drink offering, and the time*
> *of my departure has come. I have fought the good fight, I have*
> *finished the course, I have kept the faith; in the future there is laid*
> *up for me the crown of righteousness, which the Lord, the*
> *righteous Judge, will award to me on that day; and not only to me,*
> *but also to all who have loved His appearing* (vv. 6-8).

How can a Christian stay ready 'til quittin' time? How
can we keep from being caught up short? How can I
guarantee that my life won't be surprised to hear that last
shout, the voice, and the trumpet blast from heaven?
Three suggestions emerge from Paul's words.

First: *Consider your life an offering to God rather than a*
monument to men. Paul writes of being poured out as an
offering. That is a vivid word picture worth emulating.
Think of yourself as the sacrifice. Don't work on your
image, work on your offering. Consider your life as little
more than an offering poured out to God, rather than a
polished monument for men to admire.

Second: *Remember that finishing well is the final proof that*
the truth works. I find that woven into the words of verse
7:

> *I have fought the good fight, I have finished the course, I have kept*
> *the faith.*

Don't you admire people who finish? Sometimes just
finishing is as impressive as winning. Remember the
Olympics of 1984? If you do, you can never forget the
lady who ran that marathon and finally made it back to
the stadium. Remember her? She was struggling to stay
on her feet ... I mean, my family and I were watching her
on television and urging, 'Come on. Come on! Don't
stop!' As she was trying to focus on the tape, she

stumbled and fell. And we yelled all the more, 'Get up! Get up!' She did. She finally made it across the tape. She didn't win anything. In fact, she was so late it was already a done deal. For all practical purposes, the race had ended. But *she finished*. When she finally crossed over, I don't know about your family, but ours applauded and shouted in unison, 'ALL RIGHT!' You'd have thought it was our godmother crossing that line! Glory … she finished!

Plan now to finish what you have begun. It will help when the race seems extra long.

Paul concludes:

> In the future there is laid up for me the crown of righteousness, which the Lord, the righteous Judge, will award to me on that day; and not only to me, but also to all who have loved His appearing (v. 8).

Third: *Fix your eyes on the rewards of heaven rather than the allurements of earth.* There is a crown coming. So much of life depends upon the focus of our eyes, doesn't it? It recently occurred to me that as valuable as my eyes may be, they need my mind before they can do the work they must do. My eyeballs enable me to see. I am able to see *with* my eyes. But I need to use my mind to see *through* things.

Illustration: Lot and Abraham. Back in the Genesis account, uncle Abraham and nephew Lot are living together. God prospers their livestock so abundantly that they cannot stay on the same ranch. So Abraham graciously says to his nephew, 'Look, my son, decide where you wish to live. You pick it out. And wherever you and your family prefer to live, take your goods and your livestock and move. I'll take whatever's left.'

And Lot?

> *And Lot lifted up his eyes and saw all the valley of the Jordan, that*
> *it was well watered everywhere…*(Genesis 13:10)

He saw *with* his eyes how beautiful an area, how comfortable – but he failed to see *through* it. He didn't stop to think, 'This wicked place is Sodom. And Gomorrah is just as bad. Perversion is rampant. This area and these people will take their toll on my family.' Like many, he saw with his eyes, but failed to see through. Remember that. As you use your eyes to focus on the heavenly rewards, keep your mind alert so you can see through this earth's allurements.

Malcolm Muggeridge has frequently quoted the couplet from William Blake:

> *This Life's dim Windows of the Soul*
> *Distort the Heavens from Pole to Pole.*
> *And lead you to Believe a Lie*
> *When you see with not thro the Eye.*

If we committed to 'stayin' ready 'til quittin' time,' the plan isn't all that complicated. We will need to follow the model of the faithful. We will need to return to the truth of the past. As His Bride, we must proclaim the message of Christ. And in the process, we dare not fail to maintain an exemplary life.

The unbroken gold bands exchanged at weddings symbolize that two will be committed to one another – eternally. Or in the words of this chapter, 'til quittin' time. Christ has pledged Himself to His Bride forever. Have we done the same to Him? Will we – *forever?*

Study Questions

1. *Reread 2 Timothy 3:10–4:8. What challenges you most about what Paul says? In what ways would he be a good role model for your faith? Explain your answer.*

2. *One of the traditional Lenten practices is to give alms. How can you as an individual and your church do this in your context? To what extent is giving alms 'proclaiming the message of Christ'? Is it part of the message, a precursor to the message, or should it be done regardless of the message?*

3. *Discuss together specific and practical ways you can act on Swindoll's advice to maintain an exemplary life. Talk about what it means in your particular situation to:*

   Consider your life an offering to God rather than a monument to men.

   Remember that finishing well is the final proof that truth works.

   Fix your eyes on the rewards of heaven rather than the allurements of earth.

4. *Jesus is the only person who was perfectly obedient to God's plan for him. We may try and be obedient and 'stay ready 'til quittin' time' but at some point we will all fail. How do even our failures prepare us for Easter and the Second Coming?*

5. *Reflect on what you have learnt during this Lent study. What themes have impressed you most? How have you been challenged and encouraged? What changes to your life do you think God wants you to make with his help? How can the group support you?*